THE GODPARENTS' HANDBOOK

GILES LEGOOD
and
IAN MARKHAM

SPCK

First published in Great Britain 1997
Society for Promoting Christian Knowledge
Holy Trinity Church
Marylebone Road
London NW1 4DU

British Library Cataloguing-in-Publication Data

A catalogue record of this book is available from
the British Library

ISBN 0-281-05054-6

Typeset by Pioneer Associates, Perthshire
Printed in Great Britain by
Caledonian, Bishopsbriggs, Glasgow

To our parents
with love

Contents

Introduction

So you have been asked to be a godparent. Congratulations! It is a great honour. We want you to make the most of the privilege that has been bestowed on you. In this short book, we shall take you through the main issues and questions surrounding baptism and the task of being a good godparent. Do not worry if you think you are not religious enough, we will help you through some of the complexities. If you are worried as to what you can give as a baptism present or how you are going to stay in touch with your godchild, we will make suggestions here too.

In the United Kingdom the three largest Christian denominations, being the Anglican Churches (consisting of the Church of England, the Church of Ireland, the Church in Wales and the Episcopal Church of Scotland), and the Roman Catholic and Methodist Churches, all baptize infants and require godparents (sometimes called sponsors) for these children. This book is relevant to all these traditions, it is not written for any one specific Christian group.

The writers of this book are committed to an open, yet demanding faith, both in terms of mind and action. We believe that imaginative use of ceremony and the pattern of the Church's year can be invaluable ways of

1

communicating the Gospel. We want to encourage all those who are unsure and nervous about Christian belief to find a faith that provides a framework that enables life to make sense, without arrogantly claiming to have final, definite answers to all questions.

The use of the words, 'she or he' and 'her or him' could have caused us no end of problems. To simplify matters we have alternated the gender of the child chapter by chapter. To have repeatedly used she/he and her/him would have proved too clumsy.

The idea for this book emerged when on a barging holiday. We had become separated from the barge and found ourselves with a seven mile walk before we could rejoin it, which gave us plenty of time to identify the main themes of the book. Many people have helped us with the project, more than we could thank here. However, the following deserve special mention. Rachel Boulding at SPCK provided wise and thoughtful advice. Claire Moore, Sue Harwood and Alex Smith all gave invaluable advice and assistance. Leslie Houlden is a close friend and encourager to us both, in this project and in much else. Our wives, Melanie and Lesley, have tolerated hours of discussion and read parts of the manuscript. Luke Markham was born on 23 June 1996, and as a result parts of the book were written with one finger at 3 o'clock in the morning! Finally, we are both grateful to our respective sets of parents: for Giles, Dad and Mum (Ken and Angela) for Ian, Dad and Shireen. For their love we are constantly grateful. It is to our parents that we dedicate this book.

CHAPTER ONE

What are Godparents?

Millions of people in Britain are godparents, and each have their own ideas of what it is to be a godparent. This book will give you some idea of how godparents relate to Christianity and the life of the church, and will offer ways for you to build a close relationship with your godchild. We hope that you will find something new to learn about godparents – everything from the history of godparents, to their duties on the baptism day and beyond. It is a practical book; you will find lots of ideas of how to mark the occasion of baptism and how to stay in touch as your godchild grows up.

Ask the person on the street 'What are godparents?' and you will get a range of answers. Some might say that godparents are basically there to buy presents for their godchild; others might talk of the importance of supporting their godchild's family. Many think that godparents are the potential guardians for the child in the event of the parents' death. Many may not consider the religious role. This is partly because the British find religion embarrassing and partly because many people are unsure exactly how this role is carried out.

We agree with those who stress the importance of buying presents and supporting the godchild's family. These are important and should not be played down.

Families need support, especially new families who are discovering the joys of a first-born baby. Babies are exhausting and the need for support from friends is vital. Godparents can become a crucial part of that support. Many a marriage has been saved by sensitive good friends, who gently relieve the pressure at crucial moments.

Yet, it will not surprise you to know that if you get a Professor of Theology and a University Chaplain together to write a book on godparenting then they will want to show how the religious role can be affirmed and celebrated. This does not mean that we expect all godparents to be those who constantly talk about Jesus (we find them a bit embarrassing too), but we do feel that a godparent's duties cannot be separated from the promises made in the baptism service and that baptism marks a person's entry into the Church. This you cannot dodge: religion is a major element in the godparent's role.

We want to make sure that you understand all the different roles involved in being a godparent. In this opening chapter we shall look at the history, the legal status, and the duties involved, and look at the different reasons why some are asked to be godparents.

The history

Originally the need for godparents (or sponsors as they used to be called) arose when people were converting to Christianity from another religion. In the ancient world, there were many religions each with different practices and beliefs. When a member of a different religion (what Christians then called a pagan) decided that she wanted to become a Christian, she would offer herself for baptism. She would have to approach the local bishop (the person who had pastoral responsibility for Christians in a particular town) who would want to be reassured of the genuineness of the decision. The convert would then be asked to find a Christian friend who would vouch for her. This friend would undertake to the bishop that they would support the convert and ensure that she would be helped to become a faithful member of the church.

In the second century, the idea arose of having a sponsor for babies when they were baptized. In many ways it was a natural extension of the existing practice for adults. In the same way that non-Christians received help to grow into their new faith, so it was felt did a baby. Until the ninth century it was assumed that the godparents of a child would be its natural parents. Certainly it was expected that the godparents should be very close to the child. Indeed Emperor Justinian prohibited marriage between godparents and godchildren. This prohibition continues in the Roman Catholic Church today. From the ninth century onwards godparents were expected to be someone other than the natural parents. At this time there was no fixed rule as to the number of godparents permitted but in the fourteenth century it was recommended that there should only be one godparent or at most two – one male, one female.

One interesting feature of this brief history of godparents is that there is no mention of the legal role. One of the most widespread myths is that the godparents become the legal guardians of the child if its parents die. It is worth being clear about this. Godparents never had any legal responsibility for the child. The law surrounding guardians is interesting. Traditionally the child was the father's property, and so it was the father who decided all the issues relating to the child's upbringing. If the child's father was dead or absent, then it was the duty of the parish to care for the child. From a legal point of view, it was in 1891 that the child's moral welfare was first considered (1891 Custody of Children Act). Mothers had to wait another thirty-four years before their rights were acknowledged. It was only in a Parliamentary Act of 1925 that they were granted legal rights of access. Today, in cases of disputed custody it is the Family Division of the Courts that rule on the case. Even when the parents of a child determine the guardians in a will (i.e. those legally responsible for the child in the event of their death) this is not legally binding. The Family Division of the Courts will finally determine who the guardians are. If legal responsibilities concern you, you need not worry, there is no legal link between the child and the godparent.

The Churches' requirements

Each of the major Christian denominations that baptize children have their own requirements concerning godparents. In addition to this many individual priests will exercise discretion in the application of the rules. Within the Roman Catholic Church, for example, the official recommendation is that there should be two Roman Catholic godparents, one male, one female. However, in practice, many Roman Catholic priests like there to be at least one Roman Catholic godparent, but do not always insist on the second also being a Roman Catholic.

The Church of England suggests three godparents, two of the same sex as the child and one of the other sex (though parents may choose more than three god-parents). This suggestion however, may be waived at the priest's discretion. Strictly speaking all three should be baptized and confirmed members of the Church of England but most priests do not insist on this.

The Methodist Church recommends two 'sponsors' who assist the parents in carrying out their promises. The official recommendation is that one should be chosen by the parents, while the other should be a member of the congregation in which the baptism takes place, chosen by the minister. Here again, local practice can vary from place to place, depending on the minister.

Being asked

Each child needs at least two godparents (one of whom must be the opposite sex from the child). However, as we have already seen, the Church of England requires more than two godparents. Most people who have their children baptized in the Church of England choose three godparents: two of the same sex as the baby and the other of the opposite sex.

It is important to understand the role of godparents: a godparent need not be a legal guardian for the child in the tragic event of the death of the parents. The role is quite serious enough as it is with the promises you are required to make on behalf of the child. Godparents commit themselves to help bring the child up in the Christian faith. They are there to support both the parents and the child.

When a friend has a baby there is often curiosity about who might be asked to be a godparent. For parents this is a tricky decision. It is a question of selecting those most suitable for the task. Godparenting is a formal association with the child and it is an obligation that lasts a lifetime. The whole process needs to be handled with considerable tact and care. A friend in the pub, who in a drunken moment asks you whether you would like to be a godparent for his new baby, should firmly be told to consult his partner at home. Godparents should bring couples together, not divide them. Any request should be the result of thought and reflection.

Much of the rest of this chapter is concerned with looking at the different opportunities and joys that different people can bring to godparenting. However, before this is done it is important to stress that there is one thing all godparents need to be. They do need to be Christians.

Christians

It is important that those who become godparents consider themselves Christian. According to the Canon Law of the Church of England and of the Roman Catholic Church (Canon Law is the rules that govern these churches) all godparents should have been baptized and confirmed themselves. Sometimes, this can lead to problems. People who are members of the Salvation Army or the Quakers are clearly Christians, but neither group have a baptism ceremony. Some clergy will be flexible at this point. Given the promises that the god-parents are going to make, it is obviously important that the godparents are Christians.

What is a Christian?

What exactly is a Christian? This, as we shall see later, is a tricky issue. Some want to define what it is to be a Christian in a very narrow way. We want to extend the boundary much more. In the story of Jesus' life as recorded in the New Testament, Jesus had to cope with John who was upset when he heard of other disciples who were not part of his immediate group.

> John said to him, 'Teacher, we saw someone casting out demons in your name, and we tried to stop him, because he was not following us.' But Jesus said, 'Do not stop him; for no one who does a deed of power in my name will be able soon afterward to speak evil of me. Whoever is not against us is for us' (Mark 9.38–40).

Simply defined, a Christian is a person who tries to follow Jesus. Although some priests may insist that all the godparents are baptized and confirmed themselves, others will not insist on this. The important thing is that the godparents are Christians and should have some grasp of the responsibilities involved. Needless to say, those reading this book are already taking the question of what is involved very seriously.

The role of the godparent

Parents choose godparents from among their existing relatives and friends. Those who are a sister, or a 'good mate' suddenly find themselves with an additional role. It is important that you recognize your extra role. You are not just a sister or friend of the parents, with the additional title of 'godparent' to the baby. You do however bring with you the ties and links that were important for the child's parents in asking you to be a godparent. Weaving these existing ties into your godparent role will help you become a good godparent.

We shall now look at how the godparenting role fits with being a relative, or being a friend, or being married, or having children or not having children. In each case we shall look at the way the relationship should change in the light of your new responsibility.

Godparents who are relatives

Perhaps the surest and most reliable sort of godparent is a relative. The great advantage of relatives as godparents is that they are virtually certain to stay in touch. It is amazing (and often rather sad) how distance can make maintaining a close friendship so difficult. Careers and jobs may require constant movement around the country, indeed around the world. Fewer and fewer people live in the areas where they were brought up. Inevitably distance leads to changing patterns of friendship. As an example of this, look at a wedding photograph. There will undoubtedly be people on the photo with whom the wedding couple have lost contact. Indeed it is worth suggesting to all newly-weds that they list the names of those attending their wedding on the back of the group photograph. After fifteen years of marriage, there may be names of people they have forgotten!

Those godparents who are a member of the same family as their godchild have much to be thankful for. The importance of their role, for instance as an aunt, has been acknowledged, and the links have been further strengthened. They will already know much about their godchild's home life and will be able to bring this intimate knowledge to bear on the relationship. Godparents who are members of the same family as their godchild may be able to be as closely involved as a member of the same family, but also maintain a critical distance, seeing things from outside the immediate home life of their godchild.

When choosing godparents, some parents take the opportunity to create links with a distant branch of the family, for instance a cousin or an aunt may be asked. If divorce or bereavement has weakened a link with a section of the family, then godparenting can become a means of strengthening that link. If you feel this is why you have been chosen, it is important to remember this bridging role. This task can be tricky; gaps across families are sometimes the hardest ones to bridge. Being a bridge-builder in the family can become part of your particular contribution as godparent.

Godparents who are friends

When parents decide to choose a friend as a godparent, as with godparents who are relatives, they are asking for a lifelong commitment. Although some might say that your duties as a godparent are complete when your godchild is confirmed (see the chapters, 'Confirmation' and, 'What is Baptism'?) parents may well hope that you will be a part of their child's life forever.

Asking for this commitment from a friend is complex. We have already mentioned that friendships frequently depend on geography. It is hard work to stay in touch but this is all part of your role. The godparent who is some distance away can be just as precious and significant as the one who is geographically close to the godchild. Remember, getting a letter can be an exciting start to a day for anyone, not just children.

The concept of close friendship is an important one for the child to learn. By taking on this role, you will show that along with relatives, your godchild's parents have a group of people who are special. You can be one of the group who can be called on to help and support the family and child whenever there is a need.

Godparents with children

If you are a godparent who has children of your own, you might well find that your parenting experience can become an important part of your role as godparent. You will know well that having a child involves a complete change of lifestyle. With the birth of the first child, parents discover a whole set of feelings and anxieties that they never had before. If you have children of your own you will recognize and understand these feelings well.

Newborn babies are strange things: their conversation is non-existent; they cannot play games; yet they are totally demanding. Someone once said that a baby is a perfect example of minority rule. Popping out of the house with a baby, even for a short trip, involves at least half an hour of bag packing! Everything is organized around this small bundle that is completely dependent upon those around it. Often this dependence can be resented. It is a shock to discover that a newborn child demands to be the centre of its parents' lives. However, parents dominate the life of the child just as much, if not more. It is a mutual preoccupation and helping new parents to understand this can assist them in overcoming the resentment they may feel.

Children can also be totally rewarding. Babies change so rapidly; the first smile and the first word are memorable occasions. Babies however, can become the cause of great worry. When they are asleep, parents worry about cot death. When they are awake, parents worry about their baby's lack of sleep. Virtually every day occasions deep and earnest discussions between the parents: Is she okay? Is this normal? What do we next?

You will know what this is like. In the initial stages you will be needed more by the parents than the child. It is helpful to have friends who understand and friends that can help. You will also be able to reassure new parents that all babies are troublesome at times. You will, for instance, be able to show greater sympathy and understanding when the baby will not go to sleep or is teething.

Godparents without children or who are single

There are many reasons why godparents with children of their own can be a good idea. However, it is also worth stressing that those without children have a special contribution to make. There are a number of different reasons why some people do not have children. Some simply do not want children. Some are open to the possibility of children and others would dearly love to have children but cannot. All of these people can be great godparents. Any of them may find it enjoyable to get to know and love a child but still look forward to returning the child to its parents!

An important role that those without children can play is to remind those with children that there is a world and a life beyond parenting. It can be tragic to watch good, lively friends suddenly become 'Baby Bores'. All conversations revolve around the achievement of little Jenny or how exhausting little Jenny is. The 'Baby Bore' needs to be rescued. Fortunately, parents seem to have an in-built mechanism that ensures that they are deeply preoccupied with their own children; it is good to remind parents that this is not necessarily true of their friends.

Godparents who are married

Imagine this situation: your good friends who are now new parents have just asked you to be a godparent. You assume that they mean you and your partner, because after all, you are all good friends. Slowly however, they explain that they have decided to choose old friends and this does not mean your partner, because she only became a friend through you.

Because this situation can be so tricky, some parents decide to ask a couple to both become godparents. For the godparents this may make life easier because the responsibility is shared. Both make the promises at the baptism service and both accept the responsibilities. From a practical point of view it can be helpful for godparents to remind each other about the godchild's birthday and her anniversary of baptism.

Asking a couple to both become godparents is by no means the norm. For most people the process of choosing godparents is difficult precisely because there is so much choice. By the time one has a baby, there are many good and close friends to choose from. To pick both members of a couple may mean that other close friends will not be considered.

If you are a godparent to a child and your partner is not, try and understand the dilemma the parents may have felt. Asking someone to be a godparent can create problems. Those who are not asked may feel that they are not as close as they thought they were. Exclusion of a partner may lead to that person being offended; inclusion might lead to other close friends being offended.

Parents will of course be delighted if the partner of a godparent wants to be involved. If you are a godparent and your partner is not, make sure your partner does not feel excluded from this part of your life. Talk to your partner about your role as a godparent. Let them read this book. There are many ways in which they can help, advise, and support you in your duties.

The lone parent

For the lone parent, godparents can be a great source of strength. Parenting is a tricky business and is hard enough when the tasks are shared, let alone when carried out by one person. All parents have moments when the combination of tiredness and bewilderment give them the urge to scream at their baby. Lone parents may need extra support. Godparents can provide this support.

If you are the godparent to a child who has a lone parent, like those who are a godparent to a child living with both parents, you need to think about why you have been chosen for the role. Some lone parents need friends without children to maintain a link with fun and youth. This can be an important job. A godparent who is able to arrange a baby-sitter so that both parent and godparent can go out together for a child-free evening is showing good godparenting skills.

Enjoy the privilege

Whatever type of godparent you are, try to enjoy being a godparent and take the privilege seriously. You are honoured to have been asked by the parents to become intimately involved with their child. Remember that parents may have high expectations of you. They will have almost certainly have spent several hours, possibly days, trying to decide who to ask to undertake the task. Along with the privilege, of course, come certain expectations and we hope that this book will assist you in living up to these. Read the book with care, it has lots of help in assisting you to be a good godparent.

CHAPTER TWO

The Christian Faith

Later in this book when we look at the baptism service, we shall see how in order to make responses to the questions that will be asked of you and the other godparents, knowledge of the Christian faith is required. In this chapter we shall give you a brief introduction to Christianity. In order to do this, let us begin with thinking about new human life. The birth of a baby is a remarkable event. Along with plenty of pain, some stress, little sleep, and lots of anxiety, there is a delightful awareness of the simple privilege of life. A woman has carried this life for nine months; this life has slowly stretched her stomach, pushing everything else inside her body aside. Finally, with some difficulty, the baby is born.

A small vulnerable face now peers up at the proud parents. This little child is here to stay. Communication is a bit limited; the combination of grizzles and cries can mean anything from 'I am hungry' to 'I need a cuddle'. Parents spend the next few months constantly trying to guess what on earth this baby means. And over those months one spends lots of time admiring the smallness of the finger nails, the remarkable grip, and those eyes that watch awake and alert as the shadows and colours change around him.

Everyone is affected by the baby's arrival. This baby has turned two people into parents; other people become, perhaps for the first time, sisters, brothers, grandparents, uncles, aunts, or cousins. This change cannot be altered. Unlike a good holiday, where you return to life as it was before, the birth of a child stays with you. Hopefully, it is a change that will outlive you; he will provide the biological link with the generations to come. Another category of people affected dramatically by the arrival of a baby are the future godparents. It is a great honour when a couple ask their friends and relatives to be godparents.

The birth of a baby is a good reason to think about the mystery of life. We are struck by the miracle of biological evolution that can produce life. We are also reminded of the absolute truth of all life: we are all born and we all die. How do we make sense of the process? Why is there life and death?

One answer is provided by the Christian tradition. The baby is going to be baptized, and when someone is baptized they join the Christian community. But we might ask, 'What is the Christian community?' You probably already know that there is no universally agreed set of beliefs with which all Christians agree. You cannot miss the variety of different churches in your neighbourhood – the Church of England, Roman Catholic, Methodist, and Baptist Churches, amongst others. What we will do next is sketch an account of Christianity that many Christians would accept.

Christian beliefs

We will start our account by explaining exactly what Christianity is not about. It is not about believing in a large but invisible person who sits just above the clouds. Neither do most modern Christians think that God organized the universe in six days and took a rest on the seventh, or that this God explains precisely what has been done in a complicated, infallible book called the Bible. Furthermore, Christians are not preoccupied with the bliss of heaven (where we will sit around with the angels playing harps and singing hymns) or are indifferent to suffering and pain in the world. Such a Christianity most Christians would reject.

So what do Christians want to say? Christians believe that our amazing world has love right at its heart. To believe in God is to believe that love, goodness, reason and beauty are located right at the heart of everything that is. To believe in God as love at the centre of the world is quite different from believing in a God sitting above the clouds. God is personal: God is both beyond everything, yet in everything.

At this point we could find ourselves becoming sentimental, as in many sloppy American films. Here love is often identified with kissing and sex. Christians believe that love is much more complex than this. One of the words used for 'love' in the New Testament is *agapé*. This is a love which involves discovering oneself through one's relationships with others. Sometimes you find Christians talking about *agapé* as a selfless love. This is not right. To love other people we need to have our own identity. A person with no self-identity cannot love others. The tragedy of selfishness is that humans do not discover the fullness of life, and instead end up lonely. Jesus said that the second greatest commandment is that 'You shall love your neighbour as you love yourself' (Mark 12.31).

Love, understood as the creation of healthy, constructive relationships should be the goal of our lives. We need to make sure that in our busy lives we stress those things that really matter. It is very easy to get our priorities wrong in life. Careers can become more important than families, *Coronation Street* can become more important than conversations and money can end up distorting the value of friendships (those who have lots are more important than those who have none). Sometimes it is difficult for us to see that all that ultimately matters is love. Creating healthy, honest, friendships is what human beings should strive for. Furthermore, when we die it is not the end of this life, for Christians believe that love never dies. In creating loving relationships we are constructing the building blocks of eternity.

When you join the Church you are not joining a club with an agreed set of rules. You are joining a community of individuals who are committed to being more like Jesus. In the life of Jesus Christ we see love in action. Let us now examine that life in more detail.

Jesus

Jesus lived approximately two thousand years ago. He was born a Jew and brought up in Nazareth in Palestine. Almost all we know about the life of Jesus is found in the four gospels which make up the first books of the New Testament. At first sight it is puzzling why Jesus had such an impact on the world, as he only lived for thirty-three years and of the first thirty years of his life, we know practically nothing. He was executed as a common criminal by the Roman authorities on a cross. So why is Jesus so significant?

The significance of Jesus is found both in what he said and who he was. His teaching is firmly grounded in the debates of his day within Judaism. Jesus taught that the reign of God had arrived. He called the Jewish people to renewal – to rediscover the faith of the great prophets of Israel; those prophets found in the Hebrew Bible (our Old Testament) such as Amos, Isaiah, Jeremiah. He set the highest possible standards of behaviour for the Jewish people. 'Be perfect, therefore, as your heavenly father is perfect' (Matthew 5.48) is a central theme of his teaching. When communicating, he used stories and some down-to-earth illustrations to make his point. For example, when explaining how we ought not to stand in judgement over the behaviour of others, Jesus uses the illustration of a man who goes and tells a friend to remove a small speck of wood in his eye, when he is totally ignoring the massive log in his own eye (Matthew 7.3).

Virtually everyone agrees that Jesus was a profound teacher, but Christians want to say that he was more than just this. Jesus lived his life in perfect harmony with the will of God the Father. His relationship with the Father was so intimate that Christians want to claim that Jesus was God himself. This is known to Christians as the doctrine of the Incarnation. This is a difficult doctrine: how can the infinite God be identical with a finite, limited human? As we shall see later in this chapter, some Christians find this doctrine harder to reconcile with than others. The teaching of the Church, the one found in the official statements of belief (i.e. the creeds) tries to explain the problem by reference to the doctrine of the Trinity. According to this doctrine there is one God, that expresses itself in three ways. The doctrine of the Trinity sees God as Father – the source of everything that is, as Son – the human embodiment of God called Jesus, and Spirit – the continuing activity of God within the world.

Much more could be said about these doctrines, and later on in this chapter we shall briefly look at the different ways Christians understand them. However, for now, the point of this doctrine is simply that Jesus shows us what God is like. In Jesus we see a God who is committed to helping the poor and accepting everyone whoever they are. This is what is meant by love. To be a Christian is to follow Christ. Christians try to live Christ-like lives, lives that are centred on God and committed to showing the love of God to everyone.

The way of love is not easy. As we all know, the life of Jesus ended on a cross. The author of Mark's Gospel describes the crucifixion of Jesus:

> Then the soldiers led him into the courtyard of the palace; and they called together the whole cohort. And they clothed him in a purple cloak; and after twisting some thorns into a crown, they put it on him. And they began saluting him, 'Hail, King of the Jews!' They struck his head with a reed, spat

upon him, and knelt down in homage to him. After mocking him, they stripped him of the purple cloak and put his own clothes on him. Then they led him out to crucify him. . .

It was nine o'clock in the morning when they crucified him. . . When it was noon, darkness came over the whole land until three in the afternoon. At three o'clock Jesus cried out with a loud voice, 'Eloi, Eloi, lama sabachthani?' which means, 'My God, my God, why have you forsaken me?' (Mark 15.16–34).

This incredibly moving story, which is celebrated every Easter, shows us that the way of love is a difficult path. To love is to suffer with those who are suffering and it will hurt us when others are hurting. However, the story of Jesus does not finish on the cross because Christians believe that Jesus was resurrected. St Paul explains in a letter to the Church of Corinth what this involves:

For I handed on to you as of first importance what I in turn had received: that Christ died for our sins in accordance with the scriptures, and that he was buried, and that he was raised on the third day in accordance with the scriptures, and that he appeared to Cephas, then to the twelve. Then he appeared to more than five hundred brothers and sisters at one time, most of whom are still alive, though some have died. Then he appeared to James, then to all the apostles (1 Corinthians 15.3–7).

All these people, explains Paul, experienced something quite remarkable. A person who was killed by the Roman authorities is now alive. For Christians, this is the power of God at work in apparent tragedy. The resurrection shows us that our suffering and hurt will be transformed by God. We should therefore never stop hoping even when things are very difficult.

Many people find it difficult to believe in God because they do not understand why God allows suffering. If God is all-powerful and all-loving, then why is there so much suffering in this world? This is a fundamental and profound question. Nobody knows the answer to this question: we cannot know because we are not God. However, it is worth stressing that the Bible does not evade suffering. Suffering is a major theme of the Bible. In the Hebrew Bible the Jewish people suffered, they were slaves in Egypt before they were liberated into the Promised Land. They later lost the land when the Babylonians took them into exile. As we have seen, the central puzzle of the New Testament is that Jesus (the person who shows us God) died on a cross.

In so far as there is a Christian answer to suffering, it lies in the story of Jesus. Jesus was fully involved in all the problems of being human in a world of pain. Jesus had to grapple with misunderstanding and the abuse of political power by others. Jesus was a victim who died at the hands of the Roman Empire, yet all this suffering was not the end. In the hands of God suffering was, and is, taken and transformed. Pain turns into hope. Suffering can create new and exciting possibilities.

Questions and disagreements between Christians

This brief introduction to the Christian faith has already posed lots of questions. What is the precise relationship between religion and science? Is it really possible for dead people to have eternal life? We know about Jesus from the Bible, but how do we know if the Bible is reliable? Both the readers and writers of this book are still stuck with the question: Why does a good and all-powerful God allow so much suffering in the world?

These are good and difficult questions. Different Christians will give different answers. Do not imagine that there is only one answer to these questions. There is much more we could say but every Christian will stress different elements of the faith.

Disagreement is not something to be embarrassed about. Scientists disagree with each other about quantum physics, economists disagree with each other about the best way to run the economy, the police disagree with each other about the best way to tackle crime. In the same way that disagreement characterizes many disciplines, so Christians disagree about understanding God and the world. Disagreement is inevitable because the issues are complicated. If quantum physics, the economy, and crime are complicated, then how much more complicated are reflections on the ultimate nature and purpose of this world. In all these areas you have to be willing to learn from each other. Discuss and explore religious issues with others. Engage and enjoy the disagreement. One of the great things about joining the Christian community is that there is so much to grapple with.

25

One of the major issues that divide Christians is the extent to which the modern Church must believe the traditional faith found in the Bible and the creeds (i.e. statements of faith formulated by ancient Church Councils). These are the doctrines mentioned earlier, especially the doctrines of the Incarnation and Trinity. The most important creed is the one recited by many Christians every Sunday. It is called the Nicene Creed:

We believe in one God
the Father, the almighty,
maker of heaven and earth,
and of all that is seen and unseen.

We believe in one Lord, Jesus Christ,
the only Son of God,
eternally begotten of the Father,
God from God, Light from Light,
true God from true God,
begotten, not made,
of one Being with the Father.
Through him all things were made.
For us and for our salvation
he came down from heaven;
by the power of the Holy Spirit
he became incarnate of the Virgin Mary,
and was made human.

For our sake he was crucified under
Pontius Pilate;
he suffered death and was buried.
On the third day he rose again

in accordance with the scriptures;
he ascended into heaven
and is seated at the right hand of the Father.
He will come again in glory
to judge the living and the dead,
and his kingdom will have no end.

We believe in the Holy Spirit,
the Lord, the giver of life,
who proceeds from the Father and the Son.
With the Father and the Son he is worshipped
    and glorified.
He has spoken through the Prophets.

We believe in one holy catholic
    and apostolic Church.
We acknowledge one baptism for the
    forgiveness of sins.
We look for the resurrection of the dead,
and the life of the world to come. Amen.

Conservative Christians place more emphasis upon these statements of faith from the early Church, while more liberal Christians think that faith cannot be fixed in such a way. It is worth looking at this difference in more detail.

Conservative Christians believe that knowledge of God depends upon God revealing his nature and will to us. We cannot discover what God is like unless God tells us. According to conservative Christians, each generation can either create its own religious faith or accept the faith as revealed in the Bible and in the authority of an institution which has a reliable way of knowing what God is like. This institution is the Church. Conservative Christians believe that through the Bible and the received tradition alone, human beings are able to discover what God is like and what God desires us to do. The basic nature of God, as revealed to the Church, is described in the creeds. Conservative Christians stress the historic faith that tells the story of a creator God who intervenes constantly in the world and has saved the world through Jesus who died on the cross. Conservative Christians tend to believe that we need to assent wholeheartedly to the authority of the Bible and the tradition of the Church before becoming a Christian.

Liberal Christians point out that even the Church is a human institution and that human institutions are bound to reflect the assumptions and limited knowledge of each age. For instance, the Nicene Creed talks about Jesus ascending into heaven. When this was written in the fourth century after Christ, the authors were thinking of a three-tier universe, with heaven just above the clouds, a flat earth, and hell just below the ground. Now we know that the universe is not like this. Liberal Christians therefore believe that we have to believe in the creeds in ways different from the one the original authors intended. For liberal Christians, Christianity must change as the world changes and discoveries in science must alter our understanding of the traditional doctrines. For liberals, the Church must continue to reflect on the mystery of God in a constantly changing world. Things cannot be fixed and settled; God is too big and complicated for any age or institution to imagine that they have the entire truth.

There are, of course, lots of positions in between (and beyond) these two positions. Most Christians think that there is value in both approaches and many embrace both conservative and liberal elements in their thought. Most Christians value the Bible very highly, and see value in the conservative claims, yet very few Christians find that evolution presents a problem for their faith, and would also be happy to apply a liberal interpretation of the Bible on this particular point and others.

It is important to appreciate that Christians do not all agree on points of doctrine. You should not worry if you find parts of the traditional story outlined earlier in this chapter difficult to accept. As you get to know more and more Christians, you will find yourself in good company.

What about other religions?

In talking of religious faith, we should not only look at Christianity, of course, but also pause and think about other religious traditions. Christianity is the religion that dominates British culture: the Queen is the Supreme Governor of the Church of England; twenty-six of the bishops of the Church of England sit in the House of Lords; our laws are rooted in Christian values; and our major holidays (Christmas and Easter) are Christian holidays. However, although Christianity retains a dominant role in Britain, it is no longer as influential as it once was.

One of the greatest changes that has taken place over the last fifty years is the growth of other religious communities. As well as churches, we now find mosques, synagogues, and temples. Some people think that children should not be baptized, so that when they grow up they will be free to follow the religion of their own choice. There can, however, be a danger with this open attitude. In practice, children who are offered all religions but introduced to none, can end up being denied the opportunity to discover the spiritual side of life. The problem is that because all religions seem odd and strange to those outside, it becomes difficult to actually join any tradition.

Although it is important to teach children respect for the different religions in our culture, most people introduce their children to their own religion. This is the reason why if you were born in India you would probably be a Hindu or if born in Saudi Arabia a Muslim. Being religious becomes a part of your cultural identity. In the same way that language is taught from birth, so is religion. This need not worry us as it is inevitable that the place where we are born and grow up in has the greatest influence. We must all learn to respect other religions and cultures, but this does not mean that we should reject or fail to affirm our own religion and culture.

However, you might be thinking 'Well just because Christianity happens to be the historic religious tradition in Britain, that does not mean it is the best one.' You might be feeling that there is no point in believing in any old religion, as you want to be a member of the one that is true. This is another difficult and complicated question, about which much has been written and no complete answer can be given. We will however make a few comments.

First, truth in any area is difficult. Scientists from different cultures disagree about the ultimate state of the universe: in ancient Greece, Aristotle talked about every part of the universe striving for its natural end; in seventeenth-century England, Newton talked about the universe as a big machine with each part operating according to certain fundamental laws; and in the twentieth century, Einstein started to talk about the relativity of time and space. What we believe about science depends upon the culture into which we are born. The same is true of religion. We need to be careful in claming that we have the absolute truth neatly packaged in our own religious tradition. History teaches us that beliefs about 'truth' both in science as well as in religion, are often adjusted according to historical setting.

Second, the God in whom Christians believe is the God of the whole world. God's activity is to be seen in every part of the world. It is worth remembering that although humankind emerged on this globe approximately two million years ago, the first human civilizations go back only twelve thousand years. God has been active in these human communities since the beginning of time, a long time before the emergence of the Hebrew Bible. Christians believe that God is active in all human communities and many Christians would want to further affirm that God is present in all religions as they develop. These Christians have no reason to deny that God is not revealed in other religious traditions.

By bringing up their child as a Christian, parents and godparents are not therefore denying the child the fruits of other religious traditions. Rather, as Christians there is an obligation to discover the truth wherever it is found. God is God of the whole world and is able to work not just through the life of the Church, but in any situation and circumstance.

Joining a church

Getting to know Christians who emphasize different parts of the Christian faith is very important. Differences over belief become less important as Christians worship and work together. Worship is at the heart of the work of the Church. When Christians worship God they acknowledge the ultimate value of love. Through words and music Christians express adoration of God made known in Jesus. It is Jesus who embodies the things that matter most. For those unused to worship, church services can at first seem a little strange. The ritual may seem pointless and the precise order of things unclear. Do remember however that joining any organization or activity can initially seem strange. Standing in a football crowd for the first time and trying to understand the chants and reactions of those around might seem bizarre. Joining a bingo club and learning the game, discovering the rules, and enjoying the occasion, will take time. Starting anything new may seem odd, until you become used to it. In the same way the Church may well appear unfamiliar and odd. However, as you start to become familiar with the ritual and recognize the language of the prayers, so you begin to see how membership of the Church and participating in its worship can become a means of sorting out your values in the context of the love of God.

Alongside worship, there is a need for Christians to work together. If the heart of the Christian message is all about love, then of course this love must affect every part of our lives. On an individual level, we should try to be honest with those we meet (so they meet the 'real' us) and understand others (so they are the 'true' themselves with us). Instead of letting arguments get worse and worse, we should try to overcome the problem with love and forgiveness. Being a Christian is hard work because we are called to constantly examine our lives by the highest standards of behaviour possible.

Christianity is a religion that demands that our faith be put into action to create a better world. Not only should we love others as individuals, but we should change society so that it is a better place in which to live. This might mean getting involved with charities, pressure groups and political parties. Christians have a desire to change the world and make it more like the one they believe God intended.

The decision to baptize a child is a decision to introduce a child to Christianity. It is an exciting decision. For some parents and godparents it is a helpful reminder of their own decision to join the Christian Church. Use the opportunity to think about religious faith, and what values you hold dear. Perhaps, this may lead you to want to know more and to read some books. At the end of this book, we have suggested books for further reading. However, in time we hope that you will discover a greater awareness that the Christian life is about making sure that love motivates our every action.

CHAPTER THREE

What is Baptism?

Before we go any further in our preparation for the baby's baptism, we ought to think about precisely what baptism is.

Almost everybody has been to a baptism service. The baptism itself is often over quite quickly although some of the rest of the service is spent worrying about the behaviour of the baby. Will the baby cry? Will the priest drop the child at the crucial moment? With all these thoughts whirring around one's mind, it is very easy to miss the symbolism of the service. This is a pity. The baptism service is rich in imagery and it can be much more meaningful if this symbolism and imagery is understood.

At the heart of the service is the symbolism of water being poured over the person who is being baptized. This act goes back thousands of years and was given special meaning by Jesus himself.

Baptism before Jesus

The roots of baptism are both Greek and Jewish. Some of the ancient Greek mystery religions had a washing ceremony. These involved candidates being bathed with water to show that they were leaving normal society and joining the society of the gods. Baptism was also practiced among a group called the Essenes that existed two hundred years before and after Christ. Some scholars think we know something about this very strict Jewish community from the Dead Sea Scrolls. These documents were written approximately two thousand years ago, but only discovered in 1947. The Essenes believed that God was going to act decisively in Jewish history and demonstrate his power. Each member who joined the community was required to be baptized. It is possible that John the Baptist might have been attracted to this group in some way and thus brought the practice into Christianity.

Christian baptism

When Jesus was about thirty years old, he began his ministry of teaching and preaching by presenting himself for baptism by John the Baptist. John modelled himself on the great prophets of Israel who lived in the eighth century before Christ. John believed that God was about to usher in a new age and called on the Jewish people to prepare for this by repenting of their sins and being baptized. John stood in the river Jordan and called on those around him to come and get baptized in the river. John baptized by immersing the entire person in the water.

We have mentioned that according to the New Testament (the second part of the Christian Bible) Jesus was baptized by John. Matthew's gospel records it as follows:

Then Jesus came from Galilee to John at the Jordan, to be baptized by him. John would have prevented him, saying, 'I need to be baptized by you, and do you come to me?' But Jesus answered him, 'Let it be so now; for it is proper for us in this way to fulfill all righteousness.' Then he consented. And when Jesus had been baptized, just as he came up from the water, suddenly the heavens were opened to him and he saw the Spirit of God descending like a dove and alighting on him. And a voice from heaven said, 'This is my Son, the Beloved, with whom I am well pleased' (Matthew 3.13–17).

At the end of the same gospel we read of Jesus telling his disciples to carry on the practice of baptism:

And Jesus came and said to them, 'All authority in heaven and on earth has been given to me. Go therefore and make disciples of all nations, baptizing them in the name of the Father and of the Son and of the Holy Spirit, teaching them to observe all that I have commanded you; and lo, I am with you always, to the close of the age' (Matthew 28. 18–20).

After Jesus' death the Church grew very rapidly and baptism became the way of joining the Christian community. In most cases, new members were adults who had about heard the story of Jesus and wanted to follow him. In the Acts of the Apostles, we read how Peter persuaded a group of people to follow Jesus.

Peter said to them, 'Repent, and be baptized every one of you in the name of Jesus Christ so that your sins may be forgiven; and you will receive the gift of the Holy Spirit. For the promise is for you, and your children, and for all who are far away, everyone whom the Lord our God calls to him.' And he testified with many other arguments . . . So those who welcomed his message were baptized, and that day about three thousand persons were added (Acts 2.38–41).

In this case they were all adults. However, it is clear that sometimes children were baptized. In first-century Palestine, it was a common practice for a converted father of a family to require his whole household (i.e. his wife, his children and his servants and their children) to convert with him. As a result whole households were baptized. For example, when Paul and Silas were in prison, they impressed their jailer so much that:

The jailer called for lights, and rushing in, he fell down trembling before Paul and Silas. Then he brought them outside and said, 'Sirs, what must I do to be saved?' They answered, 'Believe on the Lord Jesus, and you will be saved, you and your household.' They spoke the word of the Lord to him and to all who were in his house. At the same hour of the night he took them and washed their wounds; then he and his entire family were baptized without delay (Acts 16.29–33).

As the Church started to grow, the practice of baptizing children became more common. Origen, writing in the third century, remarks in passing that 'the Church has received from the apostles the tradition of baptizing children.' Hippolytus of Rome, also writing in the third century, comments 'Children will be baptized first. All those who can speak for themselves will speak. As for those who cannot, their parents or one of their family will speak for them.' Although some of the Church Fathers (leaders of the early Church who formulated doctrine) thought it was more sensible to wait for children to grow up so they can affirm their own faith as an adult, most thought that children could be baptized if they came from Christian homes. Those who held this view thought it important that such children would be surrounded by the faith as they grew up.

As we have seen, baptism has been practised by Christians right from the earliest days of the Church. Baptism means becoming a member of the Church. But what precisely does it signify? That is the question we address next.

Significance of baptism

Much of the New Testament is made up of letters which were written by Paul to the various churches in different cities. Writing these letters to address specific problems in the earliest Christian communities, Paul uses them as opportunities to develop his theology. He is a brilliant and creative theologian. There are three passages in his letters which directly reflect on the nature of baptism.

In the first, Paul links baptism with circumcision. He writes:

> In him [i.e. Jesus] also you were circumcised with a spiritual circumcision, by putting off the body of

the flesh in the circumcision of Christ; when you were buried with him in baptism, you were also raised with him through faith in the power of God, who raised him from the dead' (Colossians 2.11–12).

Now this is a fairly complicated passage. To make sense of it, we first need to understand the Jewish practice of circumcision. Circumcision is a symbol of the particular responsibilities involved in being a member of the Jewish community. It involves the removal of the baby boy's foreskin in a special religious ceremony eight days after birth. Paul says baptism plays a similar role for Christians. Baptism is a symbol of our new life which is made possible for us by Jesus. Through Jesus we are put in touch with God in a new way. As the Jewish baby boy is symbolically welcomed into the Jewish community, so the Christian baby is symbolically welcomed into the Christian community, the Church.

In the second passage, Paul draws on another image grounded in Judaism. When writing to the Church in Corinth, Paul likens baptism to the Exodus.

I do not want you to be unaware, brothers and sisters, that our ancestors were all under the cloud, and all passed through the sea, and all were baptized into Moses in the cloud and in the sea, and all ate the same spiritual food, and all drank the same spiritual drink. For they drank from the spiritual rock that followed them, and the rock was Christ (1 Corinthians 10.1–5).

The Exodus refers to the episode in Jewish history

when the Jews were slaves in Egypt. According to the story, God sent Moses to liberate his people by leading them out of Egypt into the promised land (modern day Israel). The word, 'exodus' literally means, 'to lead out.' Paul says that in the same way that the Jewish people were liberated though the Exodus, so Christians are liberated through baptism. Baptism frees us to live a full life which is in harmony with God and with each other.

So far, the two images from Paul concerning baptism that we have looked at, have been joining the Christian community and liberation into new life. The third image of baptism used by Paul is found in his letter written to the church in Rome.

Do you not know that all of us who have been baptized into Christ Jesus were baptized into his death? Therefore we have been buried with him by baptism into death, so that, just as Christ was raised from the dead by the glory of the Father, so we too might walk in newness of life (Romans 6.3–4).

Our word 'baptism' comes from the Greek word *baptizein* which means 'to immerse'. As those being baptized are immersed in water, so they are symbolically dying with Jesus. As they come back out of the water, so they are symbolically rising with Jesus. The point to understand is that we need to let all our tendencies to selfishness and unkindness die and allow new life to come from God. This new life can enable us to discover the love that demonstrates unselfishness and kindness.

This brief survey of Paul's teaching on baptism may come as a surprise to some readers. Many people think that baptism is essential for a baby as otherwise the child goes to hell when it dies. Unfortunately, it is true that some branches of the Church have talked in these terms. As we have already seen, however, it is not an idea found in the New Testament. Further thought tells us that it also contradicts everything we believe about God. We will look at this tradition and explain why we believe it to be wrong.

Baptism, babies and original sin

Cyprian of Carthage, living in the third century after Christ, declared that infant baptism was God's mechanism for overcoming the effects of original sin. Later, Augustine, the Bishop of Hippo, writing early in the fifth century after Christ, was instrumental in promoting the idea more widely.

Original sin seems a very strange idea. According to Augustine, when the first human being, Adam, first sinned in the Garden of Eden, he passed the 'disease' of sin down the line to all subsequent humans. Augustine thought that when a baby was baptized, the guilt of original sin was eliminated, although the disease still resulted in humans doing wrong things. However, because the guilt was eliminated, heaven was guaranteed. As a consequence of this Augustine further thought that any person (including a baby) who was not baptized, was still guilty of original sin and would be punished in hell. Augustine did concede that the punishment of babies in hell would not be as unpleasant as adults who have lived a longer life and actually committed sinful acts.

Many Christians (including the authors of this book) have difficulties with the doctrine of original sin. An eternity of punishment as a result of seventy years of partially sinful human existence seems rather disproportionate. Original sin also raises theological questions about a God who is loving and good deciding to create humans knowing that many of them would end up in hell for eternity. It is manifestly unjust to suggest that a baby who is not baptized should be condemned to hell. Punishment is only fair provided that the person being punished is responsible for provoking the punishment. It is not the fault of any baby if she is not baptized. It would therefore be unfair to punish the baby.

There are very few Christians indeed who defend the doctrine that unbaptized babies are damned. Almost all Christians believe that God does not work in this way. For the rest of this chapter we look instead at some of the more constructive ways of viewing baptism. These views further develop the themes we have already identified in the New Testament.

Baptism: joining the Christian community

The decision to have a baby baptized is a decision about joining the Christian community. As we have seen, this has been the case since the earliest days of Christianity. All converts to Christianity proclaimed their faith by being baptized. Today when a baby is baptized the parents and godparents are declaring their intention to encourage the baby to grow up in the Christian community. The baby is joining a community that is almost two thousand years old and is found in virtually every country in the world.

Being part of some sort of community is very important. Human beings are social animals, we need each other. Babies are born into families; families make up villages, towns, and cities. It is good for each individual born into this world to have an immediate network of support. Babies need their parents, brothers need their sisters, friends and neighbours need and support each other. The journey of life is not supposed to be entered into and lived in isolation. Sometimes, sadly, this network of support is not present. Sometimes babies are neglected by their parents, natural family relationships break down, or economic pressures destroy relationships and communities. As a consequence mutual support is not always possible.

The Church however, should be a reliable network of support for all people whatever their situation. Unfortunately, sometimes the Church falls short of the ideal. When a child is brought to the Church for baptism, she is becoming a member of a world-wide family. Even when other support mechanisms fail, the Church ought always to be there, ready to help. This ideal is only made possible by each individual Church member being ready and willing to offer support to others when needed.

The Christian community is not simply another club. There are lots of associations that provide a social life and support. The Church is a community which believes that life should be centred on God as revealed in the life of Jesus. It is a community committed to praying for those who are its members and those who are not.

When a child is introduced to the Church, she is also introduced to the resources of prayer.

Some people are not introduced to the Christian faith as children, although some of these people are subsequently baptized as adults. It is not easy, and perhaps not appropriate, to pick up adult candidates and hold them over the font to pour water over their heads! An adult candidate for baptism stands next to the font and leans over it so that the priest can pour water over her head. The basic act, involving water, is used with the same symbolism as for babies.

Some Christians (for example those who call themselves Baptists) feel that it is not appropriate for people to be baptized until they are able to make the decision for themselves. In these Churches, baptism is only permitted for those old enough to appreciate the significance of the decision to become a Christian. Those traditions committed to 'Believers' baptism' tend to stress the importance of a 'moment' when a person decides to become a Christian. Other Christian communities place more emphasis on the need to grow into faith.

Baptism as the divine affirmation of life and new life

Earlier in this chapter we saw how one of the images used by Paul in his letter, written to the Church in Rome, is that baptism is the identification with Jesus as he died and rose again. One of the central themes of the Christian story is that God wants to transform us so that we can transform the world. Sometimes it looks as if the world is simply marked by death and decay. However, looked at another way through the death and resurrection of Jesus, God has changed the whole world. God has made this resource available to all people.

A baby is a new life full of potential. The potential of life can either be used for good or bad. The birth of every human being is a moment of excitement because birth is the start of something fresh and new. God wants each human being to come to know and live out its potential for love. In our lives we let ourselves and others down and sometimes we do not deserve this opportunity and empowerment. Newborn babies have not done anything to earn this privilege, it is a gift from God. For centuries the great majority of Christians have talked about baptism as a sacrament. A sacrament is a sign of a reality that God has given to us. In baptism water is taken, blessed and used as a sign of the reality of God's love, a love that can bring new life and new possibilities to those who want it.

Baptism's link with confirmation

In the natural course of events, babies grow into children and children grow into adults. At baptism, parents and godparents make promises to provide the child with the resources, opportunities, and encouragement to follow Christ as they grow up. As we shall see later in this book, the fulfillment of baptism is confirmation. The decision to be confirmed is one made by the child when she is older. At this later step a person 'confirms' the decision made on their behalf by their parents and godparents at baptism. We will look at this idea of confirmation and the confirmation service itself in chapter 8 of this book. It is to the decisions and promises made on her behalf at her baptism that we now turn.

CHAPTER FOUR

The Baptism Service

Soon the day of the baptism will arrive and you will officially become a godparent. This will be the day when you have a starring role. You are going to have to make certain promises. At the heart of these promises lies the responsibility to introduce the child to the Christian faith, not only in what you say but also in what you do. Earlier in this book we saw that the Christian faith is understood in a variety of ways. It is worth remembering that all Christians agree that loving every child and encouraging children to discover the importance of love is one of the greatest concerns of God.

Each of the major Christian denominations that baptize children has its own, slightly different baptism service. Although they may vary, the main components included are similar. The order of service may differ. *The Book of Common Order* contains the baptism service for the Church of Scotland and there is also a service book for the United Reformed Church (see Further Reading, p. 136). In this chapter will shall look at the eight main components that are common to the Anglican, Roman Catholic and Methodist Churches in this country. These are:

1 An explanation of the duties of parents and godparents
2 An explanation of the significance of baptism
3 A declaration that you will turn to Christ and renounce sin and evil
4 The sign of the cross
5 The baptism and a declaration of the Christian faith
6 The giving of a lighted candle
7 The welcome of the congregation

For children baptized in a Roman Catholic church, there are two additional components:

8 The prayer of exorcism
9 Clothing with a white garment.

Each of the denominations will have these main components at different points in the baptism service. We suggest that you read this chapter together with a copy of the service that will be used at your godchild's baptism. This will allow you to link the appropriate sections of the service with the commentary which we provide. We shall work through each of these components of the service in turn, and explain what is happening at each point.

1. An explanation of the duties of the parents and godparents

In the Anglican Churches in this country, godparents agree to take on three special responsibilities; to pray for the child, to set him a good example and to teach him. In the Roman Catholic and Methodist Churches godparents promise to help the parents. For godparents of all denominations, it is a good idea to take these three responsibilities as a description of what supporting your godchild and his parents involves.

First of all, you must pray. To help you with this responsibility, you will find at the end of this book a chapter saying something about prayer and suggestions that you might like to use in praying for your godchild. Prayer is important for a number of reasons. It means that in a disciplined way you express your concern and care for the child. When you pray for your godchild you should focus and concentrate on him, bringing him to the front of your mind. In so doing you should also examine your responsibilities as a friend of his parents and pledge yourself to support them too. Furthermore, prayer is a way of offering your concern to God, a way of letting God's love create further loving possibilities through your prayer. To pray for your godchild is not an optional extra but an important duty.

The second responsibility to which you have agreed is to set the godchild a good example. Adults have considerable power over children. A child's notion of what is acceptable will be determined by the adult role models that surround him. When a child is born into a violent atmosphere, it is hardly surprising that he grows up with violent tendencies. As a significant friend of the parents, you have been asked to provide a particular role model. It is obviously essential that you provide a good one.

The third responsibility is to teach the child. In the same way that you will serve as a role model for behaviour, so you will become a resource for all those questions that children have. Here you are given the responsibility to be constructive and helpful when asked those questions. The Church expects godparents to play their part in introducing the child to Christianity. We suggest later in this book that the annual cycle of remembering the life of Christ together with festivals and saints' days can provide an invaluable way of fulfilling this responsibility. In addition of course, it is a good idea to seize those inevitable opportunities that children so frequently offer, to open the child's eyes to the complexity of this wonderful world and the nature of God, in whom Christians believe.

2. An explanation of the significance of baptism

At some point in the service there may be at least one (and possibly more) readings from the Bible, or a telling of the story of how baptism is an important part of the history and life of the people of God. It is in this section of the service that the priest or minister outlines the significance of baptism. The child is becoming a member of the Church. To understand this part of the service, you need to read the chapters 'What is Baptism?' and 'The Christian Faith.' The God who is love calls on us to love others. This can be easy to say and difficult to do as it is all too tempting to be preoccupied with ourselves and lose sight of the importance of loving others. Christians believe that God in the person of Jesus can enable us to love less selfishly. Baptism is a decision, by the parents and godparents on behalf of the child, to become a member of the Church, which is a community dedicated to realizing the resources that God has made available through Jesus to transform our lives, and the lives of others.

3. A declaration that you will turn to Christ and renounce sin and evil

In some churches, you will find that these questions are directed at the parents alone; the godparents will be simply asked to support the parents. However, in the Roman Catholic and Anglican Churches the questions are directed to the godparents as well. For the purposes of clarity we shall follow the order of questions as found in the Church of England, using the *Alternative Service Book 1980*.

First of all, you are asked whether you turn to Christ. The term 'Christian' means follower of Christ. As we saw in the chapter 'The Christian Faith' Christ was a person who showed us the nature of love. In turning to Christ, you are declaring that you want to express the love of God that was shown in Christ. This inevitably leads to the second question of whether you repent of your sins. Given the importance of love in your life, you must also consider those tendencies in your life that are destructive, cruel, and damaging. Sin is just a rather old-fashioned word that sums up all these tendencies. Repenting of your sins deals with the past but you also need to promise to do better in the future. This is the third question: Do you renounce evil?

The Church is very perceptive when it comes to its analysis of wickedness. The Church sees that although we are all too painfully aware of the destructive consequences of wickedness, it can have a certain attractiveness.

For example, there is something satisfying about a good gossip, however destructive the rumours. In being called to renounce evil, the Church wants a clear declaration that you reject certain patterns of behaviour which involve dishonesty, cruelty and other destructive forces.

This is an important moment in the service. Do use the opportunity to reflect on your values. Perhaps you are aware of certain trends in your life that frighten you. Take the opportunity beforehand to talk to a priest or a Christian friend. In the same way that babies represent fresh, unsoiled life, so you can use the opportunity to create a fresh start.

4. The sign of the cross

Most services will involve a moment when the sign of the cross is made on the child's forehead. In the Roman Catholic Church, you might well be asked, along with the parents and other godparents, to make the sign of the cross on the baby yourself. This part of the service is rich in symbolism. For many people now, the cross means no more than a pretty decoration or a piece of jewellery. It is worth reminding ourselves that in actual fact it represents a cruel and barbaric means of capital punishment. As we saw in the chapter 'The Christian Faith' the cross illustrates the way that suffering and death are at the heart of Christianity. Christians are called to carry their own cross; in other words, we have to follow the way of love despite its costs. For Jesus, this meant death by the authorities of his day. Being obedient to the call and having the responsibility of love is hard work, but this is the Christian responsibility.

In some churches, you will notice that oil is used for the signing of the cross. This also has its own significance. On Maundy Thursday in most cathedrals in this country, the Anglican and Roman Catholic clergy take part in a service where they renew their ordination vows to their bishop. At this service the bishop blesses all the oil that will be used by the priests in their work throughout the following year. Oil is used not only at baptism but at confirmation, ordination and for anointing the sick and the dying. Using oil blessed by the bishop reminds us that the child is not just joining the local church but joining a community that is worldwide and spans many centuries.

5. The baptism and a declaration of the Christian faith

At some stage in the service the baby will have water poured over his head or possibly actually be dipped in water. At this point you should recall the millions of babies and adults who have joined the Church through baptism. The baby is now joining an enormous community of Christians, who have all joined through a rite that goes right back to Jesus himself. The use of water also evokes certain great themes that are found in the Hebrew Bible (for example, the Exodus – where the people of Israel were liberated from Egypt by going through the Red Sea).

In some services the moment of baptism is linked with the affirmation of the Christian faith. This might involve saying the Apostles' Creed, or simply answering some questions. If you have to answer some questions, these will involve affirming your faith in God as Trinity.

In the chapter 'The Christian Faith' we discussed the different ways in which Christians understand the Trinity. We saw how for Christians, belief in God embraces three elements. First, we are making a claim about the nature of the world. Christians talk about God as the creative force in the world. We talk about God as Father, with this creative sense in mind. Second, we believe that when we look at Jesus we are seeing God. In the person of Jesus who lived and died on a cross, we see love embodied. Third, when we talk about the ongoing activity of love in the world, we see the work of the Spirit of God.

As we saw in earlier chapters, this is a complicated theology. Being a godparent does not require that you study for a theology degree. No one expects you have sorted out everything which is involved with the Trinity. The greatest theologians in the Church did not manage that, so it would be very unreasonable to expect that of you. The words are trying to express a mystery: a mystery that tries to capture the reason why we are here and what we are intended to become. It is impossible to have everything clearly sorted out.

6. The giving of a lighted candle

In most services, you will be given a candle by the priest or minister, normally lit from the large Easter candle. Fire and light have fascinated humanity since our origins. The way the flame waves and wiggles in the air creating a small arena of light pushing back the darkness has been a rich resource for Christian symbolism.

To live in love is to live in light. The darkness represents disorder, uncertainty, unhappiness and fear. Love is that which pushes back the disorder, brings some certainty, and transforms unhappiness and fear. As you accept the candle on behalf of the child, you are accepting a symbol of hope. You are also trusting that light and love will fill that child's life, a light and love that will dispel the darkness and hate. Jesus called himself 'The Light of the World'; the candle you hold on the child's behalf reminds us that as Christians we are to shine and to draw people to the source of this light, Jesus Christ.

7. *The welcome of the congregation*

The whole point of the baptism service is that the child is joining the Church. At some point in the service, the congregation will be invited to welcome the child, to promise to pray for the child, and asked to support the child's family in this journey that they have all embarked upon.

The Roman Catholic service of baptism has two further components:

8. *The prayer of exorcism*

In the chapter 'What is Baptism?' we examined briefly the view that baptism was the moment when the stain of 'original sin' was removed. This was the view that the disease of sin, which started with the first act of human disobedience, has passed down the generations to every human being. The prayer of exorcism is a prayer that asks God to strengthen, guide and guard your godchild through the whole of his life.

There is an important point for us here. Every time you watch the television news, it is amazing how time and time again you can see the human race illustrating how destructive it can be. There seems to be an almost universal tendency to selfishness, which expresses itself in a tribalism that can destroy communities and nations. One way of looking at the prayer of exorcism is to see it as a request that the child should be freed from this human weakness that causes this sin and selfishness.

9. The clothing with a white garment

In the Roman Catholic service, just before the giving of the lighted candle, white garments are put on the child and the priest says:

> (*Name*), you have become a new creation, and have clothed yourself in Christ. See in this white garment the outward sign of your Christian dignity. With your family and friends to help you by word and example, bring that dignity unstained into the everlasting life of heaven.

The symbolism is beautiful and obvious. The child has been washed clean, by participating in the death and resurrection of Jesus through baptism. A symbol of purity is whiteness and as a sign of this the child is dressed in a white garment.

As you look at this child dressed in white it is worth reflecting on the potential of new life. Babies are full of potential. The home, family, and friends of the child will largely determine whether that potential will be realized for good or bad. The home environment is the single most important factor in the child's upbringing. A home which only knows violence, hatred, and mistrust will almost certainly produce children who are violent and full of hatred and mistrust. As a godparent you have a responsibility to be a good influence on the child. Your responsibility is to ensure that you do your best to help the child reject a sinful life and to encourage him to grow further into the new life in Christ, a life symbolized by the whiteness of his baptism garment.

Reflecting on the day

You have been part of a fabulous drama. People close to you who have had a baby have brought their child into membership of the Church. Already you are aware of the enormous change to the parents. They are different; they may have a sense of added responsibility that was not there before. You have now become a major part of that baby's life. The service might have ended, but your responsibilities as a godparent have only just begun. It is now official; you can beam with pride when someone mentions the child. You have been given a privileged status. It is one that you must take seriously.

CHAPTER FIVE

Marking the Occasion

Many people, when they think of Christianity and the task of following Jesus, think that you cannot have any fun and should not own many possessions. Individual Christians and the Church as a whole have at times helped paint this distorted picture. While over-dependence on possessions is indeed a bad thing, it is wrong to say that Christians should hate or reject all that they own. Presents, for example, are a good way of showing our love to someone. We want to suggest that much of the Christian story is about giving and gifts. Briefly, we shall touch on certain central themes and look at the way they relate to giving. Many of these themes are developed in more detail in other chapters. The human life of Jesus, his words and actions, and the teaching of the Church will all be looked at. After this, the largest part of the chapter will be spent giving ideas and suggestions for godparents to mark and celebrate the occasion of their godchildren's baptism with gifts.

The gift of Jesus

'God in human form' is a neat summary of what Christians believe about Jesus. As we saw in chapter two, when he lived in Palestine two thousand years ago, his followers thought of him as the ultimate gift: a gift of God. Christians believe that in Jesus we see God's true nature. This is a nature of love and beauty that can transform the world. Right at the heart of the Christian story is the greatest gift of all: the gift of Jesus.

Jesus and gifts

Jesus took the idea of gifts very seriously. He saw that there was much that was good in giving some people a token of your love for them. In Mark's Gospel chapter 14, we see one example of this. Here we read the moving story of the woman who poured a jar of expensive perfumed oil over Jesus just a few days before he was killed. At the time his disciples were furious because they thought that the oil could have been sold and the money given to those who were poor. However, Jesus knew that the woman's action showed how much she loved him, and that she had anointed his body for burying. He called the woman's action and gift 'a beautiful thing'.

The Church and gifts

As we mentioned earlier the Christian faith does not reject the material world. The very fact that Jesus was God in human form makes the physical fleshiness of our existence a holy thing. Soon after Jesus died the early Christians who formed the Church began to use ordinary everyday things in their worship of God. Over a period of many years the system of 'sacraments' evolved in the church. The Church of England's Book of Common Prayer calls a sacrament 'an outward and visible sign of an inward and spiritual grace given unto us'. Christians believe that just as Jesus was God in human form, the sacraments too are special ways for us to receive the love of God. In baptism, the gift of water is taken and blessed and used to wash way the past and to mark the beginning of a commitment to God.

Ideas for baptism gifts

The question 'What on earth can I buy for my new godchild?' must have been asked by most people who have been asked to be a godparent. If it is a question you have asked then we hope you will find this next section especially helpful. If it is a question you have not asked then congratulations, because your problem is already sorted out, but we hope we can suggest some other ideas that might not have occurred to you.

A second question new godparents often ask about baptism presents is 'How much should I spend?' The answer to this is not so easy. Our love cannot be measured in terms of money and neither can the tokens of our love that we give. Some presents that cost nothing in financial terms can mean everything to the person who receives the present. In the same way, presents that cost a lot of money can often be passed over without a second thought by the receiver.

Our ideas for baptism gifts are in four main categories (though some ideas could easily belong in two or more categories). We call the categories: Religious ideas; Practical ideas; Investment ideas and Treasured ideas.

Religious ideas – We mentioned earlier in the book that it is the job of godparents to teach their godchildren about the Christian faith by words and example and to be a support and friend to them as they grow up and need such help. The day of baptism itself gives a great opportunity to begin to carry out the first of these duties. There are lots of different gifts that you can give to your godchild on this day that will help you teach her about Christianity as she grows up.

We want to suggest first in this section two ways in which a godparent can contribute a gift to their godchild which will be used in the baptism service itself; by giving a baptismal gown or by giving a baptismal candle.

As we saw earlier in the chapter 'What is Baptism?', in the days of the early church nearly two thousand years ago, baptism used to take place in a large pool or river. Here, those who were baptized were totally immersed in the water. Christians, then as now, saw baptism as a new beginning, a new birth. It was traditional in those early days for the newly baptized to wear a white robe symbolizing purity. Written at that time, Paul in his Letter to the Colossians referred to this when he wrote 'You have put off the old nature with its practices and have put on the new nature.' Today this important tradition is preserved with many families having a special christening or baptism gown which successive generations of babies in the family wear at their baptism. Future godparents could easily ask if the family has a gown that it uses. If it does not, or perhaps the one it has is too small or now too old and fragile, godparents could offer to buy a gown for this very occasion. If they feel able to they could even offer to make it themselves.

Another tradition from the early Church which today's Church still carries on is that of giving the newly baptized person a lighted candle. One of the titles which Christians have always called Jesus is 'The Light of the World.' In John's Gospel we read of Jesus himself saying 'I have come as light into the world, that whoever believes in me may not remain in darkness.' In the modern baptism service this theme is echoed. Each Easter, when the Resurrection is celebrated, a large candle (called the Paschal candle) is lit for the first time. It is kept burning for the next forty days and is lit throughout the year every time a baptism takes place. It is from this Easter candle that a smaller baptism candle is lit and given to those newly baptized. This lighted candle is kept by the newly baptized and symbolizes the faith of the Christian community and reminds us that we are called to shine as lights in the darkness of the world.

Godparents have a great opportunity here to contribute to the baptism service. Although most churches will supply the baptism candle, many godparents are increasingly asking if they could be the ones who could provide the candle. This is a lovely idea and is welcomed by the churches. As a godparent you could buy a plain white candle and decorate it with appropriate symbols and words. If you make sure that the candle is at least five centimetres thick then you can carve it or paint directly onto it. Ideas for the words of the decoration include: the name of your godchild; with the date of baptism; the name of the church where the service took place. Ideas for symbols include: the cross, the hallmark of the Christian faith; a picture of water, the most important part of the baptism or a dove representing the Holy Spirit, which hovered over Jesus at his baptism.

The use of water at a baptism is essential and this provides the new godparent with a further idea for a gift at baptism. Why not buy as a present a toy that is associated with water? This will not only give your godchild lots of fun but as she grows from being a baby into being a toddler you will be able to talk about what happened on the day she was baptized. This idea of gifts associated with water will be mentioned again in the chapter called 'Staying in Touch.'

Baptism is not the point at which a new baby receives its name, as this happens when the parents register the birth of their child. It is likely however that the service is the first time that the child's Christian name is used publicly with many people present. Almost certainly the name that is used on the day of baptism is the name that the person will use for the rest of her life. This is not to be underestimated, as it is on this day that the good news about Jesus which is for all people, is given for the first time personally to your godchild. There is a long-standing tradition for gifts to be given on this day with the person's name inscribed on them. Silver christening mugs or bracelets are common gifts given by godparents. It is a good idea for godparents to ask if there is any significance attached to the child's name. It may be for instance that the child was named after another member of the family or after a figure in the Bible or a person who has been important in the lives of the parents. This might give godparents ideas for other significant gifts.

As well as mugs and bracelets, two of the other most common gifts are Bibles and service books. The gift of books of this kind is well thought out and well recommended. There are a whole host of different Bibles that can be bought as gifts. The Bible was written in two main languages: the Old Testament was mostly written in Hebrew and the New Testament was written in Greek. There are dozens of different versions of the Bible available to buy because it has been translated into English many times over many centuries by many people. If you go into a bookshop and say 'I would like to buy a Bible please,' you may well be baffled by the choice. We would like to offer some help here.

Many people when they think of giving a Bible to a child as a baptism present search the bookshops for a 'child's Bible' with large text and lots of colourful pictures. We would suggest however that a more suitable Bible to give on this occasion would be one that is not designed specifically for children. The problem we feel is one of confusing what baptism is about. Baptism is not about the end of birth, it is not a ceremony that is just for children. Baptism is about becoming a member of the Christian community and this can happen to anyone at any time in their life. Giving a child's Bible at baptism might send the message that you feel baptism is only about something that is for children. It's better surely to give a Bible that will last a lifetime; a good modern translation is best (see the 'Further Reading' section for more details). There are many modern translations that are produced with white leather covers and/or with silver-leafed edges that mark out the gift as something special – a Bible of this kind will be of use to your godchild far longer than a child's Bible. You can always buy your godchild a child's Bible when they start to appreciate pictures or learn to read, but this will be a gift that they naturally grow out of, whereas your baptism gift may well last a lifetime.

Looking for prayer books that can be given at baptism is more straightforward. In the Church of England there are two service books that are currently in use. The older of the two is the 1662 Book of Common Prayer (often known as the BCP). This book contains the historic liturgies (services) of the Church. Based on the services drawn up in the period when the Church of England separated from the Roman Catholic Church, it forms the bedrock of the world-wide communion of churches that call themselves Anglican. For giving a gift that carries a sense of history and a feeling of joining a church that stretches back centuries, the BCP cannot be beaten.

The Book of Common Prayer is of course written in the language of Reformation England. Today no one talks in the style of language in which it is written. For this reason there is also *The Alternative Service Book 1980* (usually known as the ASB). As its title implies it is a book of services that does not do away with the traditional services, but present an alternative to the book of 1662. It is written in the language of the late twentieth century. The ASB is itself due to be updated in the year 2000. If you are thinking of giving either of these service books as a baptism gift, then like the Bible, they can be found bound in special covers. As well as an unusual binding, both books can be found encased in presentation boxes. Some BCP editions have a white cover with silver-edged leaves and some ASBs are produced with a calf-leather cover.

If your godchild is being baptized into another part of the Christian community (for example the Roman Catholic or the Methodist Church) then you could give her the service book of that particular denomination. We give details of the service books of various Christian denominations in the 'Further Reading' section.

Finally, in this section we want to suggest a simple but very personal baptism gift. Most growing children make a scrapbook at some point in their childhood. Why not make them a scrapbook of their baptism? In this book you could put photos taken by you and others on the day as well as other items such as the church's news-sheet for that week with the service advertised on it. You could also add to the book by writing in what you remembered about the day, and lists of the presents that people gave to mark the occasion. Of course, this present will not be given on the day of baptism but you could give it soon after, and in later years you will be able to use it to help you talk to your godchild about her baptism day.

Practical ideas – Having a child and caring for it is an expensive task for any parent. If you are to be a god-parent to a newly born baby then it is important to realize that this period of a child's life is financially draining for parents. It may well be worth considering giving a practical gift to help your godchild's parents at this tough stage. You might find the gifts boring (can anyone really get excited about a packet of dummies or a bottle sterilizing unit?) but they will be well received and appreciated. Remember that parents who are having a second child often have 'hand-me-downs' to pass on to their new baby, but parents of a first-born child may well have to buy everything new.

Practical gifts, of course, need not all be dull and unimaginative. Children of only a few months old enjoy holding and looking at a whole range of different things (when teething they also enjoy chewing them!) Many different types of toys make good baptism presents. Not only do toys bring enjoyment, but they also help children learn basic human skills. If you are not a parent yourself or are unused to spending much time with children, it is worth checking with your godchildren's parents the suitability of your proposed toy. Some smaller and more intricate toys may not be suitable for babies and some parents may have qualms about certain types of toy (for instance they may not wish their child to have toys that promote violence or fighting).

Like toys, some clothes can also be both practical and enjoyable baptism presents. Young babies and children more easily recognize and appreciate bright, primary colours. Clothes in bold colours are therefore a good idea for a baptism present. Children about to be baptized who are older than toddler age may like to choose clothes with you. This will not only ensure they are happy with what they receive, but it may also save you the anxiety of wondering if you have bought the right thing.

A simple way of personalizing your gift is the addition of your godchild's name to the gift. A whole range of gifts can be bought with children's names on. If, however, you are unable to find a gift with a particular name on, or the name is unusual and therefore unlikely to be reproduced on gifts, then you can make or add the name yourself. We know of one three-year-old who proudly spells out his name with the help of the wooden letters fixed to his bedroom door that were given to him as a baptism present.

Investment ideas – All the gifts that we have suggested so far in this chapter are gifts which can be given to your godchild to be used immediately after baptism or soon after. We also want to suggest to you also some gift ideas that can be bought by you now, but can be put away safely to be brought out in a few years time to be enjoyed and appreciated at a later stage in your godchild's life.

It is said that a number of things get better with age. This is true: some things are at their best and need to be appreciated now, but some things are best left to mature to a time when they will be enjoyed even more. Two obvious examples which are applicable to us as godparents are alcohol and money.

Each year a large number of godparents decide to give their godchildren wine. Now don't panic, they are not encouraging under-age drinking but are aware that some wines get better as the years go by! Therefore they buy bottles of wine now for their godchildren to drink when they are adults.

We know that not all alcohol is best drunk after a long period of time. Why not ask your local wine merchant to recommend some wine (including champagne), brandy or port that will taste even better in twenty years than it does now? You could then buy a bottle or more now and give it to your godchild at a significant point later in her life. Perhaps this point could be a celebration day like her eighteenth birthday or receiving her 'A' level results (though this could be a commiseration day!). Other times might be suitable too, like the day of going to college or leaving home. We know of one godchild at university who was given two bottles of port – one he drank with friends on his twenty-first birthday and the other he drank on the day his degree result was announced (although these were only a couple of weeks apart!). Until such a day as this comes, you can either ask your godchild's parents to keep the bottle or you could store it yourself. If you have the patience you could keep one bottle to open with your godchild on the day that they have their own children baptized.

If an idea such as this worries you, you need not have doubts about the morality of giving alcohol, because the New Testament condemns drunkenness, but not drinking itself. Indeed the writer of the first letter to Timothy in the New Testament recommends him to 'No longer drink only water, but use a little wine for the sake of your stomach and your frequent ailments' (1 Timothy 4.23). Jesus too, celebrated a new marriage by drinking wine at a wedding feast (John 2.1–11, which is the first recorded miracle of Jesus' ministry).

Another way of making a gift that can be appreciated years later is through the gift of money. There are a number of ways that this can be done, many of which are simple to organize.

The two most common ways in which godparents give money are also the most straightforward. As a new godparent you can give an amount of money to your godchild as a cheque. The parents of your godchild can then spend this on things that they need for the child now, which are often the practical things that we mentioned earlier. Alternatively, if you ask them to, they can keep the money aside for later in the godchild's life. Remember that it is your gift and you should choose when your godchild receives your money.

An alternative way of giving money to your godchild to make the gift over a longer period of time. Some people choose to do this because giving a lump sum at baptism is not financially possible for them. Others choose to give smaller amounts over some years. A good way of doing this is by opening an account in the child's name and topping up the account from time to time. When the account has in it as much money as you want to give, you can give the account book to the child. It is worth remembering that an account held at a building society will earn interest on the money but an account at a bank may not. As with a single gift of money made at baptism you must decide when your godchild is to receive your gift. You might decide that the child reaching a certain age is the right time, or you might like to choose a special occasion or anniversary. Some people like to put money in the account on the anniversary of baptism and then give their godchild the amount at confirmation. The godchild can then see that each year her godparent has been thinking of her and has remembered her and the promises made on her behalf at her baptism.

More adventurous godparents (or perhaps those with a little more money to spare) give money in other ways. They may give by standing order from their bank or take out an insurance policy that will mature at an appropriate time some years on. Others may give shares in a company.

Treasured ideas – Earlier in this chapter we noted that some of the best baptism presents are not necessarily the most expensive ones. An object's value is not necessarily determined by its price.

Baptisms are often very personal and poignant occasions. This is because not only is a new stage in a person's life being celebrated, but more often than not it is celebrated with a whole range of family and friends who very rarely get together as a group. It is perhaps only weddings that provide a similar opportunity for family and friends to be together in one place at one time.

Because of the specialness of the occasion (it is an occasion that can never be repeated) it is a good time to think of making a gift that is special or unique. Because of your knowledge of your godchild and her family you may like to think what sort of gift would be special to her. If you are a member of the child's family it might be that you use the occasion of baptism to pass on a treasured family item to a younger generation of the family. Something small and simple like a photo or ornament, or something larger like a china doll or a picture, may have been in the family many years and have been passed from one generation to another. Watches and other items of jewellery might well be appropriately handed on to others at this time.

If you are not a member of the child's family or do not have an item with family associations to pass on, why not create you own treasured item? This will of course require you to spend some time thinking about what to make and then making it. When completed, however, you should be proud of what you have made and can be sure that this unique item will be treasured in later life by your godchild. Your patience and skill will be well rewarded. One of the writers of this book wrote his contribution whilst sitting on a chair made specially for him. Hanging on the wall in the same room was a tapestry made for him by a member of his family to mark a special occasion.

We hope that this chapter has given you plenty of ideas to help mark the baptism day with a special gift. We do not claim that we know all there is to know about baptism presents, and because you know your godchild's family so well, there may be ideas that we have not mentioned here that strike you as suitable gifts. Please amend or adapt our suggestions, or even ignore them entirely if you wish. The important thing is that you give a special and appropriate present for the special and unique occasion of your godchild's baptism.

CHAPTER SIX

Staying in Touch

When does your work begin?

It has been said that the easiest part of being a godparent is the baptism day itself. Making audible answers to the questions asked by the priest at the church service are the simplest things of all. The hard work of being a godparent is from that point on.

Parents choose godparents for their children for many different reasons. As we saw in chapter one, they are commonly chosen because they are friends of the child's parents. It is good for godparents to remember this because a godparent is not only concerned about his own godchild. It is important that godparents work at being a friend and support to all the members of their godchild's family. There may be times when the best thing you can do to help your godchild is to support those around him.

Until approximately two hundred years ago most people lived their whole life in the town or village where they were born. They were baptized, worked, were married, raised their children and were finally buried in the one place. Naturally then, godparents saw their godchildren very often, if not daily. Today, however, things are very different and godparents may not even live in the same country as their godchildren. This need not be a problem though; indeed living in a different place may mean that you have lots of different experiences to share with your godchild.

There are many ways in which you as a godparent can stay in touch with your godchild. In this chapter we will look at questions relating to what aspects of your godchild's upbringing you should be taking part in and what other things should involve you too. We will also describe how you will need to be aware of the changes that your godchild will go through as he grows up. At different stages in his life, to have a meaningful relationship, you may have to stay in touch with him in different ways. We will then suggest some practical and creative ideas that you can use for building and maintaining a close relationship with your godchild. Ideas are provided both for godparents who live some distance from their godchild, and for those who live close by. You will be pleased to know that many of the ideas mentioned can be used simply without much effort or hard work on your part. There may be, of course, some ideas that you do not wish to use and others that you can adapt to fit your particular needs.

What do you need to do?

Let us think about the more general issues that you will have to face. We need to be clear that you cannot simply forget the promises you made at the service. These promises are duties with practical, down-to-earth consequences. As we saw in the chapter on the baptism service, in church you promised to help and encourage your godchild to 'be faithful in public worship and private prayer, to live by trust in God, and to come to confirmation.' This is no small task; you will need to work hard at getting to know and love your godchild and to gain his trust. You will need to think of lots of different ways of expressing this through 'your prayers, your example and your teaching'.

Good godparents are not just concerned about the religious or church part of their godchild's upbringing. When we read the stories about Jesus in the gospels we see a human being who was concerned with every aspect of peoples' lives. Jesus did not just teach people about God, he made God's love known by the actions that he took. In many different places and on many different occasions Jesus spent time with people, he listened to them, he ate and drank with them, he joked with them, he healed them, he reassured them; the list could go on. The point is that following Jesus' example we should not try to separate our lives into lots of different pieces; a family segment, a work segment, a recreation segment, a religious segment and so on. As a godparent you should be interested and concerned about all of your godchild's life, not just the things that are obviously 'religious'. You do have a specific duty though to make sure God is a part of your godchild's life.

First, you should be ready to take an interest in every aspect of your godchild's life. Whatever concerns him should concern you too. Second, you will do well to remember that unless your godchild is a first child to his parents, his brothers and/or sisters will come to know you too. It can be easy for godparents to think only of their godchild and forget that other children in the same house will also be involved. Children are easily hurt and can feel left out and all your good work with your godchild can be undone if you offend a brother or sister.

Different ages, different approaches

It is a truism to say that as people get older they change. Of course, we change physically, but we also change emotionally and intellectually. You would not, for instance, expect someone to have exactly the same views on politics at ninety as they did at fifteen. Maturity involves being able to learn from what you have experienced and what you already know. Different experiences will mean that you will change your views about a whole series of issues. You may not change radically or even quickly, but change will occur. In the nineteenth century the English-born Cardinal John Henry Newman said 'To live is to change, and to be perfect is to change often.'

As we grow older we learn from our experiences of life and see the world in different ways. That greatest of all playwrights, William Shakespeare, talked of 'the seven ages of man'. He wrote that every human person has to pass through one stage at a time before they are able to move on to the next. In our own time the psychologist Jean Piaget has written about how we learn in different ways at different times in our lives. For anybody concerned with education (which includes, of course, every godparent) Piaget's work is of enormous consequence. From him we get the idea that every person can only be taught what they are ready for. From the work of modern psychotherapy and psychoanalysis we know that how we handle and manage our human needs in later life has much to do with how we were treated as a child. Freud and others demonstrate that relationships in infancy with parents and siblings will have a profound influence on how we relate to others when we are adult.

It is with all this in mind that since the 1970s an American psychologist, James Fowler, has been writing about what he calls 'faith development'. He suggests that there are a number of stages that people pass through as they grow in faith. He numbers these 0–7 and gives the approximate age at which he feels each stage occurs. The stages are not goals to be achieved but are descriptions of where people are. So that you have an understanding of how your godchild is changing as she grows up, we will describe each stage briefly.

Stage 0 relates to those aged 0–4. When writing of this first stage, Fowler realizes that it is hard to be certain what is going on in terms of faith (it is hard to conduct a question and answer session with a toddler!). Nevertheless, he sees that faith at this age is about trust. A very young child naturally trusts, but as he grows he struggles with the temptation not to trust. As children grow in this stage they gradually begin to see themselves as separate from the rest of the outside world.

Stage 1 starts at about the age of three or four and continues to seven or eight when a child's imagination runs wild. The child cannot create much order out of the chaos of the different images with which he is presented. The child can easily believe in fairies at the bottom of the garden or in Father Christmas coming down the chimney. It is vitally important at this stage that the child experiences adults as solid and dependable. This is because moral decisions by the child can only be made on what he observes of the adults around him.

Stage 2 occurs between the ages of six to seven and eleven to twelve and is also found in some adults. At this stage in growing up, the child makes big advances in learning to think for himself. The chaos of the last stage starts to disappear and the world becomes more predictable and less wondrous. This is the stage at which stories are very powerful, and the child is beginning to be able to identify with characters from a story. At this stage God is seen as some kind of strict but fair parent. This is the time of joining clubs and associations and being proud to say 'I'm in the Cubs,' the choir, class five or whatever.

Usually stage 3 occurs aged eleven to twelve through to seventeen or eighteen and is also found in many adults. At this stage the person learns to be self-aware and to reflect on situations abstractly (i.e. without needing to be personally involved). In terms of faith this is the time of conforming. It matters a great deal what others say and it is hard for the person to be too individualistic. At this stage God is seen in terms of being a friend or guide. During this time there is great emphasis on relationships, friends, teachers and others.

Stage 4 occurs aged seventeen to eighteen onwards and for some adults from the thirties onwards. This is the time of making choices and creating a personal system of values. The person at this stage is now able to look at their beliefs in a reflective and critical way and not just accept the beliefs of others. However, the belief system is supported by others, and those giving support tend to be treated as authority figures. Although the person at this stage is willing to judge their faith in the light of the faith of others, they often simplify the other's faith. Growth into this stage may take place over a very long period of time and it can be quite traumatic. It is a stage that occurs when much is changing in a person's life, whether homes or jobs or partners.

Stage 5 is rarely found in people aged less than thirty. Even for those over thirty, Fowler found that only about seven per cent of those he interviewed came to this stage. When a person has coped with the disappointments of life and faced the implications of earlier decisions, then he is at the fifth stage. Things seem more complex at this stage than before, and ideas of truth seem less tidy. This is a period when empathy with others is very pronounced and it is easy to see many sides to an issue. People at this stage are difficult to label or pigeon-hole because they see truth in other people's viewpoints. Those at this stage tend to see things as being both/and rather than either/or.

Stage 6 is normally only found in later life and is a stage that very few people move into. This is a stage where an idea of self is not important. Here people find themselves by losing themselves. Fowler gives Mother Teresa and Martin Luther King as examples of people who have come to this stage. Those at this stage see everything as bound up with everything else. The love that these people have includes the whole world and they set about trying to transform it.

What are the implications for this faith development

for you as a godparent? If you show sensitivity to your godchild's faith-age, you are more likely to be an effective godparent. Many a child complains that adults forget their age. It is easy to imagine a ten-year-old child being upset at receiving a colouring book.

Before suggesting particular ideas for you to use we want to make one important observation. When staying in touch you must remember that you want your godchild to learn from and enjoy his relationship with you. This will not be done if you ignore, or worse, do not realize what he wants. Always try to remember what it was like being a child. If your godchild is seven, then try to remember what it was like being a seven-year-old. If he is twelve, try to remember what matters to a twelve-year-old, and so on. Always try to put yourself in his position and not him in your position. It will be useful too if you think back to your childhood and remember the adults that you most liked and trusted. What was it about them that makes you remember them so favourably? Why do they stick in your mind? What was it about them that made them so important to you? If you try to call to mind these feelings, then you will give yourself a definite advantage in being an important figure in your godchild's life.

Ideas for all godparents

Some of the most effective ways of staying in touch with your godchild are also the most obvious. Every human being has a birthday and almost all human beings celebrate their own birthday (though often with less enthusiasm as the years tick by!) Cards and presents given on your godchild's birthday are a way of saying 'I'm glad you were born and I'm glad you are part of my life.' It hardly needs saying, of course, that Christmas is also a time when we make contact through meeting or sending cards and presents.

As well as Christmas, other religious festivals are good times to stay in touch. They have the benefit of not only being opportunities for you to explain the Christian faith, but because they are regular calendar events they will make sure that the time between your contact with your godchild is measured in weeks or months rather than years! Easter eggs are always well received by children but so too are presents like Palm Crosses and Advent candles or an Advent calendar. By receiving any gift, your godchild knows that you remember and love them. Godparents (indeed all Christians) have the job of showing God's love; that is, a love towards human beings which is unquestioning and undeserved. Presents such as these can be accompanied by a brief explanation of what they are and their significance to Christians. The next chapter of this book describes all the major seasons and festivals of the Church. It also suggests times when you can make a special effort to stay in touch and gives dozens of ideas as to how this can be done.

Remembering baptism together can be an excellent way of staying in touch with your godchild. On the anniversary of his baptism, you could send him cards or presents to remind him of the significance of that day. You could encourage his parents to light for a few moments the baptism candle he was given at his baptism. Like the candles on a birthday cake, a baptism candle can serve as an important reminder of the day's significance.

The present you send can either be a toy or something else you feel is appropriate. Some godparents have found that one way of linking the anniversary of baptism with giving a present, is to give presents associated with water. There are many ideas you could use at all stages of your godchild's life. When he is a baby you could give him toys for the bath. When he is a toddler you could give him armbands or a float for the swimming pool. When he is aged perhaps seven or eight you could give him goggles and flippers for the seaside (or if you have first checked with his parents, a water pistol!). A teenager might appreciate bubble bath or fancy soap. A godchild who is an adult could be given a towel for the beach. If you are able to be really generous, why not give an adventurous godchild a series of water-ski lessons? All adult godchildren, adventurous or not, may appreciate being bought a stay in a health spa with swimming pool, drinks and a jacuzzi. Likewise you could give a present that has associations with oil or water, which are also important symbols used at the baptism service.

Gifts and cards are appreciated by godchildren not only at the times described above. Perhaps you could send a present out of the blue, for no other reason than you love the child. If he asks why you sent the present, you can tell him precisely this. A generous gesture such as this, is actually the kind of love without condition that Christians see in the life of Jesus. You could give your godchild picture books, music or any of a thousand-and-one other gifts at any time, not just on special occasions.

Children from about the age of three have an amazing capacity to ask questions. Almost everything they say begins with why or where or how. Children are constantly searching for and learning about new things. Godparents can easily capitalize on this quest for information. As well as godparents finding out things about their godchildren, godchildren will want to find out things about their godparents. For instance, if you go to work then you can send them pictures of where you work and tell them the sorts of things you do. If you move house why not send them a picture of this, and perhaps for older godchildren, a simple map of where you live.

We mentioned before that birthday cards are widely sent the world over, so too is news from holiday. When you are on holiday or even just out for a day trip, you can send postcards or letters showing or describing the things you are doing. Taking photos whilst on holiday is always a good idea, because when you return home, you can send your godchild a picture or two of what you saw.

Photos can become an important part of your relationship with your godchild. As they grow up you can send them copies of the photos that you took on their baptism day. Do not worry too much if they are embarrassed by pictures of themselves as a baby, you are likely to be even more embarrassed by the fashions of the day that you were wearing! You can also ask your godchildren to swap current photos of themselves and you.

As we saw earlier, in the baptism service you promised to give your godchild help and encouragement by your prayers, your example and your teaching. Praying for your godchild can easily be forgotten in the rush of busy lives. Why not make a note in your diary or on your calendar to say a special prayer for your godchild each month? Of course, you will want to pray for them more often than that, but a mark against a certain day ensures they are never forgotten in your prayers. In this way you can tell them that you pray for them on a certain day each month (if, for instance, they were baptized on the first day of the month, then why not pray for them on the first of every month?). To help you in this, you will find prayers for different occasions in the chapter of this book called 'Prayer.'

A telephone call to your godchild can be used to follow up contact by post, or can stand as a contact on its own. Remember that godchildren need to recognize your voice as well as your face!

If you are able to, it may well be appreciated by your godchild if you can make time to take him on a day trip or day out. Cinemas, parks, zoos etc. are all obvious and good choices for such a day. The venue and location will obviously depend on such factors as time and money available and what your godchild is interested in at the time. Some godparents have used the day not only as a fun occasion but also to educate their godchildren. For instance, one godparent took his godchild to London for the day, where they were able to visit Westminster Abbey. This gave them the chance to light a candle in front of an icon of Jesus in his mother's arms, and to say a prayer for the godchild's parents together.

Earlier in this book we looked at the question of at what point, if any, your responsibilities as a godparent stop. We think that you should accept that this is a lifetime responsibility. We have already looked at ideas for a godchild going to university, but what of a god-child older than eighteen? When your godchild is an adult the contact and relationship you have with him is for you both to agree. If your godchild has left the family home, then you will no longer need to liaise with your godchild's parents in the way you once did. With an adult godchild you can arrange to do anything to which you both agree. For instance, we know of one godparent who regularly meets her godchild to go out for a meal or to go to the theatre. The relationship for them has taken on a new meaning, it is now much more equal, with them relating to each other as adult to adult, rather than as adult to child. Of course, this kind of contact is much more likely to be established if you have built up a faithful and regular contact with your god-child since he was a child.

If you and your godchild have a close relationship as adults then you may well be asked for all sorts of advice and help. In matters of career choices and job opportu-nities your godchild might look to you for independent, mature advice. In matters of relationships and lifestyle too you may be turned to as a person with whom he feels safe to talk. If your godchild decides to commit his life to another person you may feel a sense of *déjà vu*. If, for instance, your godchild has children then you may well be asked to be a baby-sitter once again. The wheel has come full circle; once you were a baby-sitter for your godchild, now you are a baby-sitter for your godchild's child!

Ideas for godparents close at hand

If you are lucky enough to live quite close to your godchild there are many ways in which you can carry out your duties as a godparent. Parents with young children often find it hard to spend significant quality time with each other. As a godparent living nearby you could offer to baby-sit for the parents (no need to wait to be asked). This is giving others help in a very practical way as well as giving you the chance to get to know your godchild. Time spent with your godchild can be very important if spent well. Taking your godchild to church is, of course, a good way of being a responsible godparent. Visiting a church at any time gives you the chance to look at the font and talk about the baptism day and what took place. Attending a church service gives you the chance to play your part in bringing up the child 'within the family of the church' (as the baptism service says). When the child is older he may well look back and remember with happiness the times you spent together.

Some older children might appreciate help with school homework and/or the chance to talk with an adult about important and sensitive things that they cannot do so easily with parents or teachers. Visiting somewhere special for a day, or perhaps even going on holiday together, are excellent ways in which the friendship of godparent and godchild can grow. Visiting the child's home and seeing him develop and mature at first hand is an experience many godparents do not get the chance to share – you are fortunate indeed.

Ideas for godparents further away

Godparents who live some distance from their godchild can have just as much influence on the life of their godchild as those who live nearby. As well as using the ideas that were suggested for all godparents, you may be able to use ideas that those godparents close at hand cannot use to such good effect. For instance, godchildren who see their godparents fairly frequently may not think there is anything special in receiving a phone call from them. Indeed, if the child is used to seeing them a phone call might seem something of a disappointment. Birthdays and other special occasions already mentioned are obvious occasions to phone, but calls at other times (especially those out of the blue) will be received with delight by godchildren.

As godchildren get older other possibilities for contact come about. Many children now have cassette recorders of their own from an early age (special toddler-friendly machines are made in bright colours with large buttons and are more able to bounce than sophisticated adult machines). This presents godparents with a chance to send a personal tape to their godchildren. The tape could include any number of a thousand-and-one possibilities: not only a spoken message but bits of your favourite music so your godchild gets to know you better, or even the sound of your pet dog barking! Technology also allows an adventurous godparent to send a video tape made with a camcorder. Increasingly, e-mail may be an important part of modern communication and if both godparent and godchild have the right equipment, then this could be an efficient, cheap and easy way for you to stay in touch.

Ideas for yourself

Being a godparent is not something that you can switch on and off as you please, and the duties you have taken on are not just responsibilities, but are also something to celebrate. You were chosen by the child's parents for the task and not someone else. Why not remember that happy day at the church by having a photo of the baptism in your home or at work? This can have three good effects: one, a photo on a mantelpiece, window ledge, desk or wherever shows to all who see it that you are proud of being a godparent and that it is an serious part of your life; two, your godchild too when he is old enough to understand will be pleased to hear things like, 'I keep a photo of you on my desk' and will know that you think of him often; three, it will be a physical reminder to you of what you promised to do for your godchild and will help prompt you to do something about these promises.

Photos can also be useful tools for prayer. If you are unable to see your godchild as often as you would like to, it is not always easy to picture them in your mind. Looking at a photo while you say a prayer for them can be very helpful. We could call this 'Praying in Touch'.

Over to you

In this chapter we have explained when your work begins and suggested some of the things that you will need to do to become and stay a good godparent. We have explained how you will need to be sensitive to the different ways of learning from and relating to the world that your godchild will experience as he grows up. We have offered ways for you to stay in touch and mentioned some ideas you might like to use for yourself at home. We hope that all or at least part of this you will find helpful as you carry out the important task of being a godparent. Despite all this, however, you yourself are the most important resource a godparent can have. Use your imagination and your time to be the best godparent you can be. No one can ask more of you than that.

CHAPTER SEVEN

The Church's Year

Spring, summer, autumn, winter, spring, summer, autumn, winter, spring . . . so goes the yearly pattern of the seasons in our lives. In the life of the Church too there is a yearly pattern which repeats itself. Like the pattern of the seasons it goes round and round, starting where it finished and finishing where it started. For this reason it is sometimes called the liturgical cycle ('liturgy' usually means the worship of the Church).

The liturgical cycle is made up of two main patterns which occur side by side. The first is the pattern which tells the story of Christ, based around the celebrations of Christmas and Easter. Because the date of Easter varies from year to year, the celebration varies a little each year. Most of these celebrations occur on Sundays. The second pattern celebrates the lives of noteworthy Christians, the saints. Because saints' days are based on the calendar year, their dates are the same from year to year (St Peter's day for example is always 29 June). Most of these celebrations occur on weekdays.

This then is what is meant by the phrase the Church's year. For some godparents the Church's year will not be familiar. Perhaps, as you become a godparent, you might want to use the opportunity to acquaint yourself with the rhythm of the liturgical cycle. However, if you find it difficult, then ease yourself in with the suggestions around Christmas and Easter.

The rest of this chapter is divided into three main sections which explain in some detail the different highs and lows of the liturgical cycle. In the first section, we will look at the seasons and main holy days of the year (the pattern celebrating the life of Christ). The second section will focus on feasts and other holy days (the pattern celebrating the lives of the saints). The final section will be concerned with other commemorations and times of thanksgiving.

One of the benefits of using the Church's year is that it provides opportunities to inform and educate. You will remember that one of the promises you made at the baptism service was to teach your godchild about the Christian faith. Other faith communities (including Jews and Muslims) have regular days of remembrance as a way of worshipping. This chapter is concerned with how the Christian community operates in a similar way.

Each of the three sections has suggestions to help celebrate and remember in this way with your godchild. There are practical ideas and activities that will help you teach your godchild that she is a member of a huge community of Christians who have celebrated both the life of Jesus and the lives of members of his church for hundreds of years. Some of the ideas are very straightforward and can be carried out without much effort or expense. Other ideas are less simple and will require you to do some preparation and planning. Though many of the ideas are well known, traditional ideas for celebration, some are new and less well known.

However, all the ideas have been used by godparents just like you before. Most of the ideas work best with younger children. Some of the suggestions can only be carried out if you live near enough to your godchild to see her, others however can be celebrated no matter how far away you live. As with the other ideas suggested in this book, please use your own imagination and your own knowledge of your godchild to celebrate in the way which is most appropriate.

The life of Christ

Most of the earliest Christians were Jewish. It was natural then that the early church adopted some of the practices and customs of Judaism. One custom was to designate one particular day of the week to come together for worship. In the Jewish system the days of the week were called the first day, the second day etc. Only the last day of the week had a title, the Sabbath. Within two decades of the death of Christ, Christians had designated the first day of the week for worship (see Acts 20.7). The first day of the week was chosen because this was the day on which the followers of Jesus first believed in the resurrection (see Mark 16.2). They called this day 'the Lord's Day'. By the middle of the second century the name Sunday was also used.

Advent

The Sunday before Advent is sometimes called 'Stir Up Sunday' because in the Book of Common Prayer and in the Alternative Service Book the special prayer for that day begins, 'Stir up, O Lord, the wills of your faithful people.' Although not the intention of the prayer, it reminds people to stir their Christmas puddings which have been made some time earlier. Perhaps you could make a telephone call today and tell your godchild about this tradition as it will give you a chance to tell them that Advent is about to begin.

Advent Sunday is the fourth Sunday before Christmas day. The word 'Advent' means coming and it is a time to prepare to celebrate the coming of Christ at Christmas. The story of the preparations for the birth of Christ are in Luke's Gospel chapters 1 and 2. To prepare for Christmas you could perhaps make an Advent wreath. This is a circle with four candles around its rim. One candle is lit on each of the Sundays before Christmas. You can decorate the circle with holly or other evergreens. Traditionally, three of the candles are purple and the one lit on the third Sunday is rose coloured.

Perhaps you could make or buy your godchild an Advent calendar. These are pictures with a set of flaps or doors which open to reveal a further, smaller picture. These calendars do not start on Advent Sunday, but on December 1st. They serve the same purpose as an Advent wreath however; reminding us what is coming soon. Try to find a calendar that tells the Christmas story rather than one that is just a pretty picture. You can also now buy in many shops a single Advent candle. Like the calendar these are designed to begin on 1 December and have a series of descending rings with the days of the month painted on. The idea is to burn a portion of the candle each day.

One of the preparations we make for Christmas is sending out Christmas cards and buying presents. Many people now draw their own cards and then either have the design photocopied or printed. Perhaps you could ask your godchild to draw a card design for you. Perhaps, you too could help your godchild buy or make her Christmas presents. This can not only be fun but will give you a chance to talk about presents being tokens of our love and that Christ is a present for the world.

Christmas

Christmas Eve

Many churches have a special service on Christmas Eve organized especially for children and called a 'Crib service'. These services are based around small figures of the people and animals traditionally believed to have been at the birth of Christ. The first crib is thought to have been made by St Francis of Assisi in the thirteenth century. Perhaps you could take your godchild to one of these services. Not only will you and your godchild get something from attending, but her parents may appreciate being able to spend some time at home alone, making last minute preparations for Christmas Day. If you are unable to accompany your godchild to this service, perhaps you could ensure that she has a crib of her own at home by sending one through the post. Christmas cribs are sold in many shops or you could make one.

Christmas Day is of course the day in the year when most paid work stops and families and friends gather together. Perhaps the best thing you can do as a godparent today is to ensure that your godchild has a happy day. Through your presents and perhaps your presence, you play your part in making the day joyful. In the New Testament both Matthew and Luke write about the birth of Jesus; Matthew in chapter 1 of his gospel and Luke in chapter 2. Remember to ask your godchild if she has put the figure of the baby Jesus into her crib.

Epiphany

The Greek word 'epiphany' means 'showing clearly'. On 6 January, twelve days after Christmas Day, Christians remember the occasion when the newly-born Jesus was shown to the wise men. You can read about this part of the Christmas story in Matthew 2.1–12. Perhaps you could make sure that the figures of the wise men are put in the crib your godchild has at home.

It was by following the brightest star in the sky that the wise men were able to find Christ in his manger. Perhaps you could tell your godchild about the stars that you can recognize in the sky. Tell her how, before modern navigation equipment, the North Star was used by sailors to find their way.

Lent

Lent is the name given to the time of forty days before

Easter (Sundays are not included in these forty days). Lent, like Advent, is a time of preparation. It is a preparation to celebrate the resurrection of Christ. It is a time to look at how we let God and other people down. It is a time for saying sorry and for preparing to make a new start at Easter. Jesus prepared for his own ministry by going into the wilderness to be alone for forty days (see Matthew 4.1–11).

Shrove Tuesday

Generations ago, the day before Lent was the time to eat up all the eggs, milk and butter kept in the house. During Lent no dairy products were meant to be eaten; instead people had to follow a simple, spartan diet. One way of using up these foods was by cooking pancakes. Perhaps you could make pancakes with your godchild. You could hold a competition to see who can toss a pancake the greatest height in the air. Few Christians today go without dairy products for the whole of Lent but most try to go without something they enjoy as an act of preparation. Perhaps you could tell your godchild what you are giving up for Lent (and why) and the two of you might like to give up something together.

Ash Wednesday

Ash Wednesday is so called because for at least a thousand years Christians have marked the beginning of Lent by making the sign of the cross on their foreheads in ash. The ash is made by burning the palms used at the previous year's Palm Sunday. Perhaps you could make a bonfire with your godchild showing her how the things that burn turn into ash.

Holy Week

Palm Sunday

On the Sunday before Easter Day, Christians remember the occasion shortly before Jesus' death when he rode into Jerusalem. He rode on a donkey with the crowd cheering him and throwing palms they had cut from trees together with their cloaks at his feet. You can read an account of this in Mark 11.1–10. In churches today you will find small crosses made from palm leaves given to each worshipper as a reminder of this event. There may also be a procession around or in the church recalling the procession of Jesus and his disciples into Jerusalem. Perhaps you could pick up an extra palm cross at church today to give to your godchild. Perhaps you could go for a walk together.

Maundy Thursday

On the night before he was killed, Jesus gathered his disciples around him and had a final meal with them. Before this 'Last Supper' Jesus washed his disciples feet to show them that a master is not greater than his servant. During the meal he then blessed a loaf of bread and broke off a piece for each of them to eat. After the meal he took a cup of wine and gave it to them and they all drank from it. Jesus said to his disciples that evening that the bread represented his body and the wine represented his blood. You can read an account of this in Mark 14.12–25. Christians remember this event every Sunday and every other time that the Eucharist is celebrated. This service is also called the Mass, Holy Communion and the Lord's Supper. Perhaps you could make some bread with your godchild, or send her some flour through the post, to remind her of the Last Supper. Because Maundy Thursday reminds us of the need to serve others, perhaps you could ask your godchild if you could do something for her: perhaps her room needs tidying for example.

Good Friday

This is the most solemn day for the Church. It is on Good Friday that Christians remember Jesus' trial, crucifixion and death. The story is told in all four Gospels but the one that is most widely read in churches today is from the Gospel of John chapter 18 and chapter 19.1–37. Christians try not to work today but use the time to pray, think and read about Jesus' final hours. Traditionally many Christians fast today although it may not be advisable for those who are young, old or ill. Most Christians will eat simple, small meals that contain no meat. Today is the day when hot cross buns are eaten. These brown buns have a white cross on the top and are made with spices to remind us of the spices used to anoint Jesus for burial. Perhaps you could send your godchild some money to buy some hot cross buns. Remember to ask her to buy the buns the day before so the shopkeeper does not have a reason to open on Good Friday.

Holy Saturday

Just as we have Christmas Eve, so some people call this day Easter Eve. Today is the day that we remember that Jesus' body was kept in the tomb. The piece of scripture particularly important for today is Matthew 27.57–end. Perhaps you could make an Easter Garden with your godchild. This is a model consisting of a hill with three crosses on top in one corner and a tomb with its entrance blocked in another corner. It represents the hill of death where Jesus was crucified and the tomb of new life and resurrection. The model can be decorated with flowers and other plants you have picked together.

In the early church Easter was the time for baptism of new converts and the children of church members. Today too, many baptisms occur on Easter Day or at a special service on the night of Easter Eve (called the 'Easter Vigil'). It is at this service that the new Easter candle is lit for the first time. From this large candle, smaller candles are lit throughout the congregation who say to one another 'The light of Christ.' We said earlier that it is this Easter candle that is used at every baptism that takes place in the church for the next year. Perhaps you could light the candle given to your godchild at her baptism or talk about what happened on that day. Perhaps you could send your godchild a candle or candle holder today.

Easter

Easter Sunday

This is a day of great celebration for all Christians. It is the day that the women and then later the disciples discovered the empty tomb and rejoiced that Jesus had risen from the dead. The versions of what happened on that first Easter morning are slightly different in all four gospels but the longest account is that of Matthew 28.1–11. On this day Christians celebrate that the cross was not the end of the story about Jesus and that new life was found in him after his death. Just as people give each other presents at Christmas, so too many people give eggs at Easter. You can use the giving of eggs to talk to your godchild about the new life of a chick and link this with the new life discovered by Jesus' friends at Easter. Perhaps you could also organize or take your godchild on an egg hunt. This is simply done; just hide a few small eggs in the back garden or somewhere in the house and children can be amused for hours.

Easter Monday

Many Christians in this country and the rest of Europe go for a walk on Easter Monday. Some walk part or all of the way to their own cathedral. This tradition is probably linked to the story of Jesus walking on the road to Emmaus after the resurrection, with two of the disciples. You can read this story in Luke 24.13–35. Perhaps you could go for a walk today with your godchild.

Ascension

In the first chapter of The Acts of the Apostles we read that for forty days after the first Easter the risen Jesus spent time with his friends and disciples. The writer of Acts tells us that after this Jesus left them and ascended into heaven. Perhaps you could take your godchild to the top of a tall building or a hill. Perhaps you could send them a balloon through the post and ask them to blow it up, let it go and watch it float up to the clouds. Tell them that they don't have to think of Jesus shooting into the sky like an astronaut. Instead they can think of him as being the 'top man'. Explain to her that when we talk of someone being top of the class or coming top in their exams we do not mean it literally but that it is picture language. Because Ascension Day is forty days after Easter Day, it is always celebrated on a Thursday.

Pentecost

Ten days after Ascension the Church celebrates Pentecost (it is always therefore on a Sunday). In the second chapter of Acts we read that some time after the Ascension the disciples were meeting together when the Holy Spirit came to them giving them the strength to carry on the work that Jesus had begun. When the Spirit came it was like a rushing wind, and this sound was heard by many people in Jerusalem. The Spirit looked like tongues of fire and rested on each of the disciples and gave them the ability to speak in other languages. Many foreigners who were in Jerusalem at the time were thus able to hear the word of God spoken to them in many different languages. Perhaps you could light a fire or candle with your godchild to see what tongues of fire look like, or you might like to light a barbecue instead. Perhaps, if it is a windy day, you could fly a kite together or if unable to meet, you could give your god-child a kite a few days beforehand.

Trinity Sunday

The next Sunday after Pentecost is Trinity Sunday. Unlike all the other celebrations of the Church's year mentioned in this section of the chapter, Trinity Sunday is not a day connected with the life of Jesus, but is a celebration of the way we know God. On this day the Church gives thanks that though we worship one God, God has three parts, the Father, the Son and the Holy Spirit. Perhaps you could think and talk with your god-child about things associated with the number three. Perhaps you could send her a clover leaf which though one plant has three leaves. If your godchild is musical perhaps you could listen together to a piece of music that is counted in bars of three.

Pentecost season

The time from Pentecost to Advent is called the season of Pentecost or of Trinity. Each Sunday from now on is numbered after Pentecost or Trinity. In many churches the altar on which the Eucharist is celebrated and the vestments which the clergy wear are green. For this reason some call this time a time for growth. Over the summertime so much of the natural world is green and in full bloom. It is appropriate therefore for Christians to think about how they themselves are growing physically, intellectually and spiritually. Perhaps you could talk with your godchild about how you have grown in these ways and tell her that humans should never stop growing and maturing. Perhaps you could visit the country or a park and see the beauty of the natural world and see how plants and trees grow and adapt throughout their life-cycle.

Advent again

Depending on the date of Easter, the end of the Pentecost or Trinity season finishes about twenty weeks later. The liturgical cycle never stops but keeps rotating and re-telling its story. After a year of hearing of and thinking about the life of Jesus, from the news of his mother's pregnancy to his death, and the news of his resurrection, the Church's members begin to hear afresh the story of the life that shapes their lives. For every church member, each year brings the opportunity to hear a part of the story in a new way. Perhaps something will occur to them that they had never thought of before. A phrase or incident may take on a new meaning or reveal a new depth. A story from the life of Jesus may speak to a church member in a way it never has before because of new experiences that have occurred to them personally since they last heard the story. There is always something to be learned and gained by hearing the story again and again. The life of Jesus cannot be told too often and when it is told it is important that nothing is missed out and that Christians are forced to hear even the parts they would rather not hear or think about.

The Lives of the Saints

The tradition of remembering in a formal way the lives of certain Christians is almost as old as Christianity itself. In the early church it became common to visit the burial places of those who had taught the faith or been killed because they were Christians, and whilst visiting, to celebrate the Eucharist on their tombs. In non-Christian Rome, to commemorate the birthdays of those who had died, people used to visit the tombs of the dead and have a meal there in their honour. These two customs came together and soon Christians were celebrating the Eucharist on the anniversary of the death of certain prominent Christians. From about the fourth century onwards more people began to attend these celebrations and it became necessary either to build a church over the tomb or to hold the celebration in a nearby church. Soon churches began to celebrate the lives of saints who were not buried locally, and later, important Christians from the New Testament were also remembered.

Today, the process by which certain Christians after their death can be called 'saints' is quite formal. In the Roman Catholic Church the Pope declares who may be called a saint only after a long legal enquiry. In the Orthodox Churches a meeting of the bishops of one particular area has this power. In the Church of England no new saints have been declared since the time of the Reformation, when the Church broke away from the jurisdiction of the Pope, although the ASB of 1980 gave the names of several women and men from recent centuries it thought worthy of commemoration.

The new calendar of the Church of England also gives the names of more people it suggests should be specifically remembered.

We now want to suggest some ideas for remembering some of the lives of these Christians with your godchild. There are literally hundreds of saints remembered by different Christians throughout the world so we have selected just a few to consider, and placed them in order from January to December. Lists of the saints are printed in many books (Prayer Books are especially helpful). We hope you will find out about some of the other saints that we do not list here and use them as inspirations for your own Christian life. Perhaps also you could discover which saint is commemorated on your godchild's birthday or anniversary of baptism, and tell her about this person's life.

St Agnes (21 January)

Agnes is one of the most famous of all Christians who was put to death for her faith by the Romans. She died in Rome in about the year 304 aged only twelve or thirteen. A church was built over her tomb, and by 354 her name was already included in the lists of martyrs celebrated in the liturgical cycle. Little else is known about her. Perhaps you could talk with your godchild about how difficult at times it is to be a Christian. Tell her how lucky we are to live in a country and time in history when people are not persecuted for following Jesus.

The Conversion of St Paul (25 January)

In the very earliest time of the Church a man called Saul persecuted Christians. Following a dramatic incident he became a Christian himself, changed his name to Paul and devoted his life to travelling around the Mediterranean and Asia preaching the gospel. Paul is the author of a number of Letters in the New Testament addressing particular difficulties various Christian congregations had. Perhaps you could read the story of his conversion in Acts 9.1–22 and then take your godchild on a day trip or journey. Alternatively, you could visit St Paul's Cathedral and look at the inside of the dome decorated with pictures showing scenes from St Paul's life. Maybe you could write a letter to your godchild and tell her of your own travels.

St Alban (22 June)

In about the year 209 the first known Christian martyr in Britain was killed. Alban was a pagan soldier living in the Roman town of Verulamium (now St Albans in Hertfordshire). He gave shelter to a priest who was being pursued. After seeing the priest's life of prayer and humility, Alban became a Christian. Soon, however, the priest's pursuers found where he was hiding and came to take him away. Alban put on the priest's cloak and gave himself up in the priest's place. The judge ordered Alban to be flogged but no amount of torture would make him renounce his new faith. He was therefore put to death. Perhaps you could visit St Albans Cathedral and see the shrine built there. Alternatively, you could go shopping together and you could buy your godchild a coat or other item of clothing.

St Thomas (3 July)

Often known as 'Doubting Thomas'. Thomas was the disciple who needed to see the wounds in the hands and body of Jesus before he could believe in the risen Christ (see John 20.24–29). Ancient Christian tradition has it that Thomas was the person who first took Christianity to India. Perhaps you could think with your godchild about how doubt is not a bad thing, and that the opposite of faith is not doubt, but certainty. If you both like spicy food, you and your godchild could go out an have an Indian meal, or maybe stay at home and have a take-away.

St Francis of Assisi (4 October)

The son of a rich merchant, Francis rejected the life of luxury and swapped clothes with a beggar and lived a simple life of poverty. Others soon joined him and so he founded an order of monks who devoted themselves to a life of humility and generosity. Francis was especially well known for his love of animals and the natural world. Perhaps you could send some money to your godchild and ask her to choose a charity to whom she could make a donation. Maybe you could visit a zoo today or spend some time helping your godchild care for her pet animal.

St Teresa of Avila (15 October)

For many Christians the life of this Spanish nun is an inspiration. In her own lifetime Teresa was known for her wise and elegant written advice. She advised people in all positions in society: popes, kings and ordinary lay-people. She spent much time in quiet contemplation and prayer. However, Teresa also led an extremely busy and active life. In founding seventeen convents through-out Spain, she travelled widely and was noted for her common sense and efficiency in everyday matters. Perhaps you could take your godchild to visit a quiet place, away from the hustle of her ordinary life. Alternatively, you could talk with her about places that are special to you and that you visit for reflection and relaxation. You could send her a book or a picture of a quiet mountain range. Perhaps you could send her the prayer written by Teresa reproduced in the 'Prayer' chapter of this book.

St Cecilia (22 November)

Little is known for sure about this woman who lived in Rome in the second or third century. Legend says that she converted her husband and his brother to Chris-tianity and that, like them, she herself was put to death for her faith. It is certainly the case that from at least the sixth century onwards, Christians in the west have recognized Cecilia as a saint. An account of her death speaks of her singing to God in her heart and for this reason she is regarded as the patron saint of musicians. Perhaps you could take your godchild to a concert today. Maybe you could talk with her about your favourite pieces of music and ask her to play you some of the music she likes. Alternatively, you could send her a tape or CD of some music.

Other commemorations

In addition to the two patterns celebrating the life of Christ and the lives of the saints, the Church also sets aside other days to pray for other concerns. Many different churches, either locally or nationally, have their own list of these days. As with the lives of the saints, they are too numerous to all be mentioned. We will mention however just five such occasions that are widely observed in Britain.

Week of prayer for Christian unity

Christians all serve and worship one person, Jesus Christ. When praying to his Father, Jesus prayed that all those who followed him would be one (see John 17.20–23). In the northern hemisphere of the world today, most Christians dedicate the week of 18–25 January to praying especially for Christian unity. In many places Christians of different traditions come together to pray and worship at a common service. Readings and prayers are put together in a special booklet that individual Christians can use in their own homes throughout the week. Perhaps you could take your godchild to one of these special services or to a service in a church different from her own church. Maybe you could tell her some of the things that the churches are all agreed upon or some of the things that divide them.

Mothering Sunday

The fourth Sunday in Lent is referred to by many Christians as Mothering Sunday. The precise reason why this day was chosen is not known but a number of suggestions have been put forward. Some suggest it is so because it was common in many parts of England for children living away from home to go and visit their mothers on this day. Some believe that this is the day when people used to visit their cathedral or mother church on this day. Others think the day got its name because one of the Book of Common Prayer readings for the day is from Galatians 4 which has the words 'Jerusalem . . . which is the mother of us all.' Whatever its origin it is the case that most churches now have a special service or include special prayers for mothers on this Sunday. Perhaps you could pick some flowers with your godchild to give to her mother. Maybe you could help her choose and buy a present for her mother. Alternatively, you could take her to visit her cathedral or the church where she was baptized. Perhaps you could tell her some of the things you most love about your mother.

Rogation

The three days before Ascension Day are set aside by the Church to pray especially for God's blessing on the fruits of the earth. The origin of this is in the fifth century when the Archbishop of Vienne in France instructed members of his church to pray that earthquakes and other disasters did not occur in their region. Perhaps you could plant some vegetables with your godchild today. If you are unable to visit her, perhaps you could send her some seeds to plant. Maybe you could send her a bible passage such as Deuteronomy 8.1–10 to read.

Harvest Thanksgiving

Around the beginning of October each year, different local churches give thanks for the safe gathering of the harvest. In the Old Testament the Jewish people were required to celebrate the first fruits of the harvest (see Exodus 23.16). Celebrating what we have is right, but Jesus told us not to forget that there are other important things to remember too (see Luke 12.16–31). Perhaps you could buy some tinned or packet food with your godchild to give to a charity that works with those who have to sleep on the streets. Maybe you could harvest some of the seeds or plants that your god-child planted at rogation and eat them together. You could ask your godchild if they celebrate harvest at her school.

Remembrance Sunday

The First World War officially ceased at 11 a.m. on the eleventh day of the eleventh month of 1918. Countries who had been involved in the war soon came to observe two minutes' silence at this time in each subsequent year. After the Second World War, people in Britain started to remember those who had died in these wars on the Sunday nearest to 11 November. Many local churches have a special service on this Sunday. Perhaps you could take your godchild to visit a war memorial or another place associated with war. Maybe you could take her to see an older person who could tell her of some of the sacrifices and the horrors of war. Alternatively, you could talk with her about some of the wars that are taking place in our own day.

If you follow some of the suggestions in this chapter then they will help you to stay in touch with your godchild. Many relationships with children lapse into a routine where the conversation never gets beyond 'How are you?' By taking advantage of these ideas, you can build a friendship that explores your godchild's hopes and fears. They will give you the opportunity to gently widen your godchild's perspective. You can encourage some reflection on literature and politics. If from your godchild's early years you start creating a friendship of substance, then as your godchild grows so your friendship will deepen. As well as making an appropriate contribution to her life, so you will find your own life enriched.

CHAPTER EIGHT

Confirmation

Becoming a godparent is a great privilege. You are a significant part of a child's life. Your godchild has only a few godparents, and you are one of them. This is unalterable: it will always be true. From the day the child is baptized to the day you die, you will always have this privileged status and responsibility. However, you will be pleased to hear that when your godchild gets confirmed, then in one sense your responsibilities are over, because confirmation is the point at which a person takes on the promises made on his behalf at baptism, for himself.

Talking about religion

It is important that you play your part in helping the child to make his own decision about Christianity. Children have an enormous appetite for religion. From the age of about five onwards, children are able to have thoughtful conversations about religion. Sadly, we have become a culture embarrassed by religion; general conversations forbid conversations about, 'sex, politics, and religion'. This is a pity, because the human spirit needs to think about religion and enjoys thinking about religion. Making space for your godchild to talk about religion is one of the most important contributions you can make. One of the reasons for this is that religion needs thought: an unthinking childhood faith will not survive into adulthood, unless it grows and matures.

One of the major reasons for adult confusion about religion is the commonplace childhood confusion between God and Santa Claus. Santa is simply a childhood myth that you are expected to reject as you grow older. Santa is a bit of fun at Christmas time. God should be completely different. To believe in God is to believe in the ultimate triumph of good and love over evil and hatred. Life is not simply this moment, but part of a greater picture. To ensure the child distinguishes Santa and God, you need to slowly introduce increasing sophistication into his faith.

For a first picture of God many people have an idea of a big daddy in the sky who is looking down from heaven. Such a big God can rapidly become grotesque or indecent (he is watching us everywhere, even when we are undressing) and incompatible with our scientific knowledge of the world (where is this God located and what sort of body does he have?). These are the sorts of reasons that undermine belief in Santa Claus (how on earth can he get around every house in the world in one evening consuming vast quantities of sherry and mince pies?)

It is a major development in the human understanding of God when we move beyond a big-person image. In the book of Isaiah, the prophet stressed how unlike the rest of creation he believed the creator of the world must be. Isaiah could not reconcile the source of everything that is with one of the objects within that creation.

Although it is true that we can have a relationship with God, and in that sense God is personal, it is wrong to imagine that the relationship with God is just like any other relationship. It is helpful to introduce gently some complexity into your godchild's understanding of religion. Ask them challenging questions: get them to think hard about what they mean, but remember that they are not yet adults, so the questions should be appropriate to their age. This not only ensures a growing maturity in the way God is understood, but it teaches the godchild that questions are not to be feared. Questions are a legitimate way of discovering the truth and that truth has nothing to fear from questions.

As the child grows into a teenager you can expect a period when many things, including God, are rejected. The godparent should enjoy this period. Let the godchild explore doubt, think about other religions, and denounce the hypocrisy and vice that are evident in the Church. It is possible that this state of mind will stay with the godchild. If so, then your responsibilities are to pray and be faithful. Continue to enjoy the questions and disagreement. You should not worry about the ultimate attitude of your godchild to religion: leave that to God. Your task is to keep the issue of religion alive, for God has a special way of getting through.

For most teenagers, rebellion in the area of religion, as in much else, is part of the process of growing up. Godparents need not be too concerned about this: their godchildren can now become conversation partners. It is important that you let your own thoughts about religion change as a result of the insights provided by your godchild. We can all learn from each other. Part of your role is to encourage openness, and openness is taught by example. As the godchild starts work or goes to university, then the godparent should be ready to learn. In a changing world, younger generations always have much to teach us.

Young adults are quite unpredictable. Experimentation is part of being young. Naturally, some experimentation should be discouraged. Drugs, for example, can seem attractive but in fact prove to be destructive. However, experimentation in ideas is rarely harmful. If you godchild decides reincarnation makes sense, then your responsibility is to listen, understand, and make sure you are informed about the belief. But keep asking the questions. Some Christians have attempted to reconcile reincarnation and Christianity (for example, the early-Church theologian Origen), while most others feel that this is not possible. Your responsibility is to encourage serious and informed reflection. Perhaps this might involve finding some books for your godchild to read, or directing him to a good sensitive priest who knows about these issues.

It is worth pointing out that thus far we have stressed the religious role: you are the adult in the child's life who has an official licence to ask the child about religion. Naturally, you can only do this provided you have a good and healthy relationship, and take an interest in every aspect of the child's life. In our experience, godparents can often enjoy a much broader relationship with the child than the parents can. As a young adult discovers the complexities of sexuality, it can be to the godparent that he turns. Let a broad rich friendship develop, one which is built upon trust and confidentiality. In this way, the religious dimension is naturally interwoven with the rest of life.

Most often the decision to get confirmed is the result of many factors. Your responsibility is to be one of the good friends who has encouraged a thoughtful faith to emerge and develop. When the matter of confirmation is raised, some godparents find themselves in the embarrassing position of encouraging their godchild to take a step that they themselves have not yet taken. If you have not been confirmed yourself, this might be the time to consider it.

The confirmation service

In traditional Anglican and Roman Catholic theology, confirmation is seen as the fulfilment of baptism. Confirmation brings out all the potential intended at baptism. There is a slight awkwardness here as neither church wants to imply that the original baptism was not complete. As we saw in chapter three, baptism carries enormous significance: the candidate turns to new life as he joins the Church. Baptism is the sacrament of initiation. Baptism is frequently referred to in the New Testament, although confirmation is never mentioned.

In the early Church, confirmation was not originally performed as a separate rite but was part of baptism. The separation of the two arose from an logistical problem. In the earliest times of the Church it was the bishop, as chief pastor of the local Christian community, who administered baptism. However, due to the rapid growth of the Church, this became impossible. Bishops therefore authorized their priests to baptize people, on the understanding that the bishop would 'confirm' them at a later stage. Once separation of baptism and confirmation became widespread, it was felt that the bishop's confirming should only take place when the candidate was aware of the decision that he was making.

Today, as for centuries, there is much discussion amongst Christians about confirmation. While many Christians feel the practice outlined above is a good one, others feel that the Church should practise only believers' baptism (that is baptism should only be administered to people who are old enough to make decisions on their own behalf). Other Christians feel that infant baptism should continue, but children should be allowed to play a much fuller part in the life of the Church, and should be permitted to receive communion before confirmation, for instance (this is the practice in the Roman Catholic Church).

Baptism and confirmation remain central to the life of the Church of England and the Roman Catholic Church. Although it is true that baptized children are full members of the Church, it is considered necessary for the baptized person, when he is ready, to express his own commitment to the Christian community. Ideally, this should happen when the person concerned is able to have a clear understanding of the decision that is being made. The candidate for confirmation should not therefore be too young. Before confirmation there should also be some discussion with the Bishop's pastor in the locality, the priest, as to what is involved in a person committing himself to the Church. This will involve the priest explaining the teaching of the Church and what it is to be a member of the Christian community. The candidate must be in a position to make an informed response to the questions asked of him at confirmation.

When you made the promises at the baptism service, you did so on behalf of yourself and on behalf of the child. At confirmation, godchildren make these promises for themselves. The confirmation service uses the same promises: 'Do you turn to Christ? Do you repent of your sins? Do you renounce evil?' The same questions about God are asked: 'Do you believe and trust in God the Father, who made the world? Do you believe and trust in his Son Jesus Christ, who redeemed the world? Do you believe and trust in his Holy Spirit who gives life to the people of God?' Instead of the godparents providing the answers, this time the godchild is able to do so.

Confirmation is the point at which godchildren choose to continue in the Church for themselves. It can take place anytime between the ages of eight and eighty or older, though it most often takes place between the ages of eleven and fifteen. Normally, confirmation is preceded by a preparation course. This often sounds much worse than it actually is. People expect a series of long lectures by the priest. In actual fact, most priests use it as an opportunity to encourage a group of people to talk about their faith, raise their doubts, and discuss the demands of being a Christian. Often confirmation classes use videos and music to make them more interesting. Many people reflect with affection on their confirmation classes. Given busy lives, it is difficult to create the space to reflect in a sustained way on life and faith. The very fact that these classes are required is the reason why some people find it is the only time they have to think deeply about their faith.

In the Church of England, confirmation is normally the way in which a person is admitted to Holy Communion. The reason why we say 'normally' is because members of other Christian churches are welcome to receive communion in Anglican churches, and sometimes, children or others preparing for confirmation are permitted to receive Holy Communion.

The person responsible for conducting the confirmation service is a bishop. Bishops are the chief pastors of the Christian community. They are responsible for overseeing groups of local churches and providing the guidance and support to help the priests and people living in the area (called a diocese).

When the confirmation service occurs it is important for you to attend. This should be a priority. You will have played a fundamental role in bringing your godchild to confirmation. Unlike the baptism, you will have nothing to say, all you have to do is beam with pleasure as your child is confirmed.

Confirmation: part of a journey

Confirmation is part of a journey. The Church of England expects those who are confirmed to find time to read the Bible, pray daily, and regularly attend Holy Communion. Other churches expect a similar commitment. It is here that a godparent can once again be of help. It is customary to mark the event with a gift. All the suggestions made at baptism for 'Marking The

Occasion' can be adapted for confirmation. Probably the most common gift is a bible or prayer book. You might also want to suggest to your godchild some bible reading notes to help them discover the Bible better.

Those who get confirmed relatively young will find it a long and interesting journey. Almost certainly there will be moments of unbelief and confusion. Most human lives are touched with some tragedy: illness, early death, separation, or divorce touch most families at some stage or other. It is through the difficult times, that a sensitive godparent will be needed. Do not worry if you are not on hand to provide answers or solutions: for many human problems such things do not easily exist. Your role is much more simple: you are there to help, support, love and pray, and to let the love of God, as revealed in Jesus, be revealed in your life too. For older godchildren a good godparent becomes less like a parent and more like a good friend.

CHAPTER NINE

Prayer

As we have seen in some of the previous chapters of this book, prayer is a crucial part of the Christian life. From the earliest Christian times, prayer has been central to the Christian life. Like Jesus, many of the early Christians were Jews and so were already familiar with regular patterns of prayer, whether alone or with others. This final chapter will explain the value of prayer and how you can pray. It will also give you some prayers that countless numbers of Christians have used and loved for many years and that you may find of help yourself.

What is prayer?

In the broadest sense prayer is an entering into communion with God. We could say then that the whole of a believer's life is a prayer. Most often though, when the word prayer is used, it is taken to mean the time set aside to focus on God. People use different symbols to help them become more aware of God. For Christians, the greatest symbol is a person, Jesus. Although Jesus lived in a different time and a different place from us, reflecting on his life and how the power of God was at work through him, can give us pointers as to how we should live our lives. Christians pray in the power of the Spirit, through Jesus Christ, to the Father.

When should I pray?

St Paul wrote, 'Pray without ceasing' (1 Thessalonians 5.17) that is to say, there should never be times in our lives when we abandon the need to pray. We should be clear that prayer is not something we do only when we are in trouble or feel we want a favour from God. Prayer is not an easy way out of a difficult situation with no effort involved on our part. As Jesus showed in living his life, God needs to act through human situations and through individual human beings. Prayer is more properly seen as the power of God helping us do things for ourselves and others.

When we pray we do not need to be in a special place or acting in a special way. We can be aware of God anywhere and everywhere. God is as much to be found in a busy supermarket as in a quiet country church. We can pray whilst walking down the high street in a group or sitting on top of a remote hillside alone. Wherever and whenever we pray we should not feel that we have to use special words or a special language. Prayer should not be unnatural or false, it should be as normal as chatting with the person next to you or with a well-trusted friend.

When it comes to the act of praying, different people have different experiences. Some find prayer easy and have an active and full prayer life. However, some may find that prayer is hard or will not come easily. Others still, see prayer as a place of last resort, that is used when disaster strikes. Like most things, prayer needs to be learnt, it takes time to feel comfortable about praying. If you are not used to praying regularly, you may find it helpful to begin to spend some time in quiet meditation. Think of a person or an issue that concerns you and place it in the context of eternity. As you become more comfortable with prayer, allow your prayer time to embrace other people and situations.

How can I pray?

It is easy for us to feel that prayer is something that just involves us talking and God listening. If we feel this we are mistaken, because prayer is not simply about us demanding God's attention but is also about us being attentive to God. Prayer is not just saying 'God I want you to do this' but it is also 'God, what is it that I should do?'

As well as praying in a spontaneous way in normal everyday situations, it is important that Christians regularly find space in their lives to have special, quality time for prayer. In the accounts we have of Jesus' life we read of him regularly strengthening his relationship with God through times of prayer. He did this in two ways. He found time to be alone to pray (for instance, Luke 22.39–41). He also prayed with others. Not only did he pray with his disciples (Luke 9.28) but he also took part in the regular worshipping life of the community (Luke 2.41–49). We too should develop a prayer life like this. It is important that we not only make the time to be alone with God to pray, but that we also make the time to worship with other Christians and hear together the stories of the Bible and share in the Holy Communion (1 Corinthians 11.23–26).

Types of prayer

Because our prayers are expressions of what we feel and desire we use different types of prayer in different situations. The prayer used by new parents as they stare in wonder at their newborn child is very different, for example, from the prayer used by a soldier sheltering from enemy fire. Let us briefly look some different types of prayer.

(a) *Adoration.* Adoration is a resting in the presence of God. Although we normally use words and symbols in our prayers, adoration may not need these. Perhaps words cannot adequately describe our feelings about God. Many people find different gestures useful in prayers of adoration; bowing, kneeling, even lying face down. Adoration is focusing on and celebrating the qualities the Christian believes about God. Some find it useful to focus on a different quality on a different occasion. For example, one time you could focus on God as all merciful, another time God as all loving or all good and so on.

(b) *Confession.* Prayer of confession is where we acknowledge where we have gone wrong. Confession is the recognition that as human beings we sin; that is we fail and fail again. We sin not only by saying or doing bad things but also by failing to say or do good things when we should have. Having recalled our sins, prayers of confession then ask for God's forgiveness. But that is not all; though the slate is wiped clean, so to speak, we also have to pledge ourselves to doing better in the future and thus becoming more like Christ.

(c) *Petition.* For many people this is the most common type of prayer used. Petition is asking for something we desire for ourselves. People from many different religions and cultures have prayed for almost everything imaginable. There is a danger that we may only selfishly ask for what we think is in our best interest. This is wrong and before Christians pray these prayers we need to be aware of our dependence on God and interdependence on all other human beings. We should pray not just for material things but also for the qualities which will enable us to become better people. Jesus knew that praying to the Father is not about demanding that certain things be done but rather it is 'Father . . . not my will but yours be done' (Luke 22.42).

(d) *Intercession.* Prayers on behalf of another person, another group, or for the world are prayers of intercession. Like petition they are prayers of asking. Like petition too, intercession is not simply presenting God with a shopping list of requests and demanding that they be granted. Prayer requests are about not just words but actions too. God works through human beings and we should, and must, expect to work to help others and build the Kingdom of God here on earth.

(e) *Thanksgiving.* It is all too easy for us to take the good things in life for granted. Prayers of thanksgiving enable us to express our gratitude. Often, we can forget the power of God in our daily lives and ignore all the blessings we receive. We should offer thanks not only for the things that we have received but also for the blessings received by others (see 1 Thessalonians

126

5.16–18). The greatest Christian thanksgiving of all is the Holy Communion or Eucharist ('*Eucharist*' is the Greek word for thanksgiving), where Christians remember and give thanks for the life, death and resurrection of Jesus.

Familiar words

Much of this chapter has been concerned with the prayer that we make in our own words. As we said earlier it is important that the words we use in prayer are natural and feel comfortable. There is a lot to be said however for also using prayers that are familiar and that other Christians have used before us. Many of the prayers used in a church service for example may have been used by countless millions of people around the world over many centuries. Using these familiar words can have a number of benefits. These prayers remind us that the Christian community to which we belong is wider than our own particular local church. Certain prayers have been cherished by others who lived before us and may well be cherished by those who live after us. There may also be times in our own prayer life when we cannot find the right words to express what we feel or we feel that we cannot pray at all. At these times also, well-loved and well-used prayers can play a useful role.

Prayers for godparents

We finish this chapter, and indeed this book, by suggesting some prayers for you to use. You will find prayers here for different times of the day, for different times of your godchild's life as well as prayers for different moods and feelings. Some of the prayers are prayers taken from the common worship of the Church, others are prayers written by the saints or other prominent Christians, although most have been written especially for this book. As with everything else that we have suggested, please use and adapt the prayers that suit you best. Please also try to use some of the other prayers too, you may find that you come to value these as others have done before. We hope that you will find the prayers helpful to you in fulfilling your duty to help and encourage your godchild 'by your prayers, by your example and by your teaching' and that they will also help you personally in your own prayer life. As a preparation for prayer you may like to read the teaching that Jesus gave his disciples on how to pray (Matthew 6.5–11).

Adoration

Blessing, praise and glory be to you O God. You are the beginning and the end, everything that is and everything that shall be. Your goodness is greater than I can measure or imagine. Blessing, praise and glory be to you O God.

Confession

O ever loving God I confess to you that I have failed you through failing others and failing myself. In your loving compassion, forgive me all those wrong things I have done, and those good things I have not done. In your tender goodness bring me back to the way I should follow, the way of Jesus Christ, friend of sinners.

Petition

Eternal God, in my blindness I do not see when I go wrong, in my deafness I do not hear the cries of others, in my dumbness I fail to speak when you require it. O Divine healer, unblock my eyes, my ears and my mouth and give me the gifts I require to live according to the example of your Son, Jesus Christ.

Intercession

O God of infinite mercy, have compassion on all people, hear our prayers and grant us what you know we require. O God of all wisdom, give us the sight to see where others need help. O God of all power, give us the gifts to bring your healing to the world.

Thanksgiving

Glory be to God, for all the opportunities and blessings that enrich our lives. Glory be to God, for all the strength and happiness we receive from those around us. Glory be to God, for all the encouragement and example given by those who have gone before. Glory be to God, now and forever.

Morning

Into your hands, O God, I commit myself this day. May

I feel your Spirit with me always and when the day is done, may I rest secure in the knowledge that I have lived to your glory, putting the needs of others before myself.

Evening

Watch now, dear Lord, with those who wake or watch or weep tonight, and give your angels charge over those who sleep. Tend your sick ones, O Lord Christ. Rest your weary ones. Bless your dying ones. Soothe your suffering ones. Pity your afflicted ones, and all for your love's sake. (Leonine Sacramentary)

Baptism

O God of love, whose Spirit brings new life to the world, bless (*name*) soon to be baptized. Give her joy and gentleness, wisdom and courage her whole life long, and may she live and grow in the knowledge that your love reigns over all things.

Godchild

Loving God, thank your for the blessing I have received in having (*name*) entrusted to my care. May all those close to her watch over her and protect her. May she grow up rooted in love, loyal in faith and thirsting for life, for the sake of Jesus Christ.

Godchild's family

Come, O Spirit of God and rest in the hearts and
  the home of (*name*)'s family.
May your light banish all darkness,
your love overcome all evil,
your peacefulness calm all strife,
your hope transform all fear.
This I ask in the name of Jesus Christ, the light
  of the world.

Godparents

O God, the Father of all humanity, bless all who make
your love known to the world through their work as
godparents. Give us a tender care and a loving spirit and
guide our lives, that we might guide theirs and so bring
them to see the love of your Son, our Lord, Jesus
Christ, the friend of all.

Confirmation

Praise be to you O God who has given us life,
Praise be to you O God who has given us love,
Praise be to you O God who has given us faith,
May (*name*) who is to be confirmed in this faith,
  love her neighbour as herself and
proclaim by word and deed the good news of
  your Son, Jesus Christ, our Lord.

Christ's work

Christ has no body now on earth but ours, no hands but ours, no feet but ours; ours are the eyes through which to look out with Christ's compassion to the world; ours are the feet with which he is to go about doing good, and ours are the hands with which he is to bless the world now. (St Teresa of Avila)

Dedication

> Christ be with me, Christ before me, Christ
> behind me,
> Christ in me, Christ beneath me, Christ above
> me,
> Christ on my right, Christ on my left,
> Christ where I lie, Christ where I sit, Christ
> where I arise,
> Christ in the heart of every one who thinks of
> me,
> Christ in the mouth of everyone who speaks
> of me,
> Christ in every eye that sees me,
> Christ in every ear that hears me,
> Salvation is of the Lord,
> Salvation is of the Lord,
> Salvation is of Christ,
> May your salvation, O Lord, be ever with us.
> (St Patrick)

Peace

Lord, make me an instrument of your peace.
Where there is hatred, let me sow love,
Where there is injury, pardon;
Where there is doubt, faith;
Where there is despair, hope;
Where there is darkness, light;
Where there is sadness, joy.
O divine Master, grant that I may not so much
    seek
To be consoled, as to console,
To be understood, as to understand,
To be loved, as to love,
For it is in giving that we receive;
It is in pardoning that we are pardoned;
It is in dying that we are born to eternal life.
    (Attributed to St Francis of Assisi)

Further Reading

We recommend all of the following books to help you know more about Christianity and the task of being a good godparent.

John Barton, *People of the Book?* (SPCK, 1988/95)
A well written book that examines what authority the Bible has for Christians and the Church.

Richard Burridge, *Four Gospels One Jesus* (SPCK, 1995)
A clear, solid and thoughtful introduction to the four gospels.

James Fowler, *Stages of Faith* (Harper and Row, 1981)
The first of a number of books by the same author looking at how faith develops as human beings grow older.

Michael Fuller, *Atoms and Icons* (Mowbray, 1995)
An introduction to the meeting of science and religion. The author demonstates that these two ways of seeing the world are not incompatable.

George Guiver, *Everyday God* (Triangle, 1994)
A short and down-to-earth book inviting the reader to see God in all things and offering help in responding to God in prayer.

Margaret Hebblethwaite, *Motherhood and God* (Chapman, 1984)
An account of the pain, humour and joy experienced in motherhood. This easy-to-read book can help all godparents better understand how God is found in human relationships.

Richard Holloway, *Anger, Sex, Doubt and Death* (SPCK, 1992)
A brave and passionate book, written by a Bishop, that tackles the issues in the title with honesty and clearsightedness.

Gordon Jeff, *Am I Still A Christian?* (Triangle, 1992)
Examines some of the questions most often asked by people about Christianity and offers ways of making sense of these.

Sean Kelly and Rosemary Rogers, *Saints Preserve Us!* (Robson, 1995)
Gives details of the lives of literally hundreds of saints.

Diarmaid MacCullock, *Groundwork of Christian History* (Epworth, 1987)
A potted history of Christianity and the Church, from the time of the first Christians to our own day.

Ian Markham (ed.), *A World Religions Reader* (Blackwell, 1996)
For those interested in knowing more about other faiths, this book presents the world's major religions (including secular humanism), while leaving the reader to make her own assessment.

The SPCK Book of Christian Prayer (SPCK, 1995)
A large and wide-ranging book that offers prayers from all Christian traditions, stretching back centuries. Thousands of prayers are included offering the right words for thousands of situations.

Peter Vardy, *The Puzzle of God* (Fount, 1995)
A clear introduction to some of the philosophical questions about the existence and nature of God. One of a series of books by the same author (others include *The Puzzle of Evil*, *The Puzzle of God* and *The Puzzle of Ethics*).

Tom Wright, *The Original Jesus* (Lion, 1996)
An extremely clear introduction to the person of Jesus, his message and the world in which he lived.

If you intend to give your godchild a Bible or a service book at any point the following details may be of help to you.

Holy Bible, New Revised Standard Version, Anglicized edition (OUP, 1995)
One of the latest translations of the Bible. It makes use of modern scholarship and modern English usage.

The Alternative Service Book 1980 (SPCK, Clowes, CUP, 1980)
Contains all the modern Church of England services (including the service of baptism), as well as readings and prayers for Sundays and all the major festivals and saints' days.

The Book of Common Order (St Andrew Press, 1994)
The service book of the (Presbyterian) Church of Scotland.

The Book of Common Prayer (OUP)
The traditional service book of the Church of England, valued by generations of English Christians.

The Methodist Service Book (Methodist Publishing House, 1975)
The service book of the Methodist Church, this book has the orders of various services including Holy Communion and baptism.

The Sunday Missal (Collins, 1984)
The Sunday service book of the Roman Catholic Church in England and Wales. Contains special prayers and readings for the Church's year as well as the order of services such as marriage and adult baptism.

The United Reformed Church Service Book (OUP, 1989)
Like the other service books mentioned, this book contains readings, prayers and services for a number of occasions.